Cross Talking

A Daily Gospel for
Transforming Addicts

MARK E. SHAW

Cross Talking
A Daily Gospel for Transforming Addicts
By Mark E. Shaw

Copyright © 2010
All Rights Reserved

Cover Design by Melanie Schmidt

ISBN: 978-1-885904-84-3

Printed in the United States of America
By Focus Publishing
Bemidji, MN 56601

DEDICATION

To my faithful wife, Mary, and our four children: Mark, Sarah, Rachel, and Michael

To my parents, Ronny and Sandra Shaw, and my brother, David, and his wife, Tammy

To my many ministry partners at Truth in Love Ministries: Jason Cooke, Shirley Crowder, Sharon Ryce, Max Campbell, Jack Schreiner, Hal Parks, Jim Lowery, Michael Fargarson, Barry Bruce, Sharon Stephens, Nancy Kimsey, Brad Tollison, Chris Burns, Rick Whitehead, Bill Dill, Anthony Austin, Don Olvey, Michael Olvey, Brian Stockard, and Jeff Young, who serve the Lord by helping hurting souls

To my "mom" in Minnesota, Mrs. Jan Haley

And to those struggling with any type of "addiction," God has the answers and power to enable you to overcome!

CONTENTS

INTRODUCTION

At many "recovery" and self-help meetings, "cross talking" is not allowed. "Cross talking" at these meetings can be simply defined as "a dialogue between two individuals, excluding all others." It occurs when someone addresses the last speaker directly. The idea is that it inhibits open sharing and freedom to express opinions. Likewise, at many secular meetings, "cross talking," or talking about the Cross of Jesus Christ, is also denied. Higher Powers can be talked about in a generic way but not the Highest Power, the Lord Jesus Christ. This type of "cross talking" is not encouraged though it is the only true source of transformation in overcoming any addiction.

In this devotional, "cross talking" is encouraged so that you do not conform to the world's ideas but are transformed by the Holy Spirit and God's Word. Romans 12:2 states: **"Do not be conformed to this world, but be <u>transformed</u> by the renewal of your mind, that by testing you may discern what is the will of God, what is good and acceptable and perfect"** (emphasis mine). One of the central messages of Christianity is that God wants us to "be transformed" into a new creation in Christ Jesus. 2 Corinthians 5:17 states: **"Therefore, if anyone is in Christ, he is a new creation. The old has passed away; behold, the new has come."** These passages are important because this transformation is both an immediate occurrence at salvation (2 Corinthians 5:17) *and* an ongoing process of growing in Christ after salvation (Romans 12:2). The command in Scripture to be transformed applies to all people struggling with "addiction" problems. My primary reason for writing this daily devotional and other books on the topic of "addiction" is that the Lord wants you to be transformed from being an "addict" (and it applies to being addicted to anything really) into being like His Son. In other

1

words, your identity is in Christ if you are a Christian, and your purpose is found only in the Word of Christ.

Early in the last century words such as "addiction" or "alcoholism" in American culture were non-existent because people thought of the problem as a moral choice and a sin issue. The idea of alcoholism as a "disease" became popularized in the 1930's and now is a theory that is commonly accepted as "truth" by most addiction professionals and those who are battling this deadly problem. How quickly things change in our culture! The danger of calling this sin a "disease" is that it points people away from the forgiveness of Christ for all sins, even those of drunkenness. I urge you to think about this problem differently than our culture, the world, and Satan, who love calling it a "disease" rather than a "sin." For a more in-depth study on the biblical approach to addiction, I recommend you read my book, *The Heart of Addiction: A Biblical Perspective*.

God wants more from us than just "recovery," which implies self-improvement. "Recovery" is a good word. After surgery, one is placed in "recovery" for a time so that physical healing and improvement may occur in the body; however, for spiritual healing, God has a better word. God wants us to be "transformed," or changed, into the likeness and image of Christ. Our new life in Christ looks nothing like us when we are in our flesh. Just improving the flesh is not God's best for us; He wants us to be completely different than we once were. It is a spiritual change brought on by the power of the Holy Spirit. Notice the word "transformed" in 2 Corinthians 3:18: **"And we all, with unveiled face, beholding the glory of the Lord, are being <u>transformed</u> into the same image from one degree of glory to another. For this comes from the Lord who is the Spirit"** (emphasis mine).

A "transformation" is God's answer for any and all types of "addiction" and it is only found at the foot of the Cross where Jesus was crucified. This transformation is a lifelong process which begins when we are no longer thinking the way the world thinks, but instead are thinking about and viewing life correctly—as God thinks and views it. This new way of thinking comes from saturating our minds with Scripture. The Holy Spirit works in partnership with the Word of God. I encourage you to pray and utilize this booklet as a personal daily devotional, couples devotional, or in a small group of Christians in transformation. You may want to read it over and over for several months so that it will teach and remind you of God's perspective to transform you as you overcome your "addiction." My prayer for you is that you will allow God's Word to renew the thinking in your mind, experience the love of the Holy Spirit when you read, and then do what the Lord leads you to do—all for His glory to be manifest in your life.

Mark Shaw

Is This Book for Me?

"Let no one say when he is tempted, 'I am being tempted by God,' for God cannot be tempted with evil, and he himself tempts no one. [14] But each person is tempted when he is lured and enticed by his own desire. [15] Then desire when it has conceived gives birth to sin, and sin when it is fully grown brings forth death" (James 1:13-15).

I want to let you in on a little-known secret: Everyone struggles with some type of "addiction." Shhh! You don't have to repeat this. Now you might be thinking, "I'm not on any drugs. I don't even drink alcohol very often. Therefore, I can't be called an 'addict'!"

Well, what is really meant by an "addiction"? There are probably millions of types of "addictions" and the truth is that you are dealing with at least one of them. How do I know? Because I know your heart and its tendency toward pleasing yourself first before pleasing God and others. There are desires in your heart for pleasure, work, sleep, sex, alcohol, drugs, spending money, hobbies, sports, scrap-booking, e-mail, texting, acquiring antiques, and a million other things that you place as first priority in your life and are willing to pursue no matter what the cost.

These temporal pursuits can be good things in and of themselves. These "things" are not the problem. Your heart is the problem. External things are not the primary cause of "addiction." In reality, nothing external is really the root issue because the source of the problem lives within you; it is called your "flesh" or "sinful nature."

In the verses quoted above from the book of James, your *desires* are your number one enemy and lead to all types of "addictions." Desires conceive and give birth to sin that ultimately results in *death*. That death can be physical but it can also be the death of the relationships that mean the most to you.

Our "addictive" desires do not fulfill us. They do not solve problems and most often create relational ones. God wants us to live in a close, intimate, and loving relationship with Him and others. That is His desire for you, and your "addictive" choices will only lead to separation from Him and from loved ones both now and possibly in the next life. And it is ultimately your choice.

Are you "addicted" to something right now? In other words, what are you thinking about and wanting more than anything else in the world? That desire is your "addiction" and will consume you if you do not ask the Lord to intervene by the Holy Spirit in accordance with the truth of God's Word. Begin reading and ask the Holy Spirit to reveal His truth to your heart. By His power, God will transform a willing heart that yields to Him and cries out for change!

Day 1
ADDICTION'S BIBLICAL NAME (PART 1)

"They served their idols, which became a snare to them" (Psalm 106:36).

A young boy wandered around his neighborhood whistling and calling for his dog. A kindly neighbor, wanting to help, asked the boy, "Did you say his name is Killer? Is he a Doberman or a Pit Bull or what? Should I be afraid of your dog?" The boy shook his head and said, "Naw, you don't have to worry; he's a Chihuahua."

POINT TO PONDER: The name, or label, given to something can mislead others when it is not accurate. By using correct biblical names and descriptions, all kinds of "addicts" will begin to understand addiction and the solution for addiction from God's perspective.

"Addiction" and "alcoholism" are two of the many words the world uses to describe the problem of the heart the Bible calls "idolatry." Why does the world call it something different than the Bible? The answer is simple: the world has no Savior. The world denies the existence of sin because they have no answer for "addiction" when it is called "sin;" therefore, the world describes the problem as "addiction," or "alcoholism" for the person who chooses to abuse alcohol.[1] Furthermore, the world primarily views the problem as a biological one, meaning that a person has a "disease" and becomes physically dependent upon a toxic substance like drugs or alcohol. While the problem

---

[1] I put these words ("addict" and "addiction" or "alcoholism") in quotation marks because they are worldly terms and not biblical. These terms imply that a disease has overtaken someone and it can never be overcome; but we know that by the power of Christ it can.

can manifest its presence in the physical realm, since drugs, sex, alcohol, cutting, gambling, and other types of addictions have physical consequences, the heart of the problem is rooted in the spiritual. Even secular self-help groups acknowledge "addiction" and "alcoholism" as spiritual problems in addition to describing the physical consequences.   However, the world wrongly teaches that "any god will do" in their secular, so-called spiritual fellowship. As Christians, we know that only Christ will do. He Himself said in John 14:6: **"I am the way, and the truth, and the life. No one comes to the Father except through me."** Christ alone is the answer to all "addictions" when you understand that He gave His life upon the Cross to die for all sins, including the properly diagnosed sin of "addiction" which is better termed as "idolatry." Idolatry and sin are only overcome by the same resurrection power that raised Christ from the dead. Likewise, God will raise you from a dead lifestyle of addiction and sin to a newness of life only found in Christ.

PRAYER: "Lord Jesus, show me how my idolatrous heart has been a snare in my life so that I can overcome my "addiction."

Day 2
ADDICTION'S BIBLICAL NAME (PART 2)

> **"The time that is past suffices for doing what the Gentiles want to do, living in sensuality, passions, drunkenness, orgies, drinking parties, and lawless idolatry"** (1 Peter 4:3).

A forty-year old woman, who loved to eat ice cream, complained of feeling sick and physically weak for several months. She visited her doctor for a checkup, and was diagnosed with adult-onset diabetes and high blood pressure. After hearing his instructions which included no more ice cream, her response demonstrated her idolatry of the desire for ice cream. She loudly exclaimed, "What?" as she could not fathom living without ice cream "every once in awhile," and she believed her life was "not worth living without sweets." She left the doctor's office planning to ignore the doctor's orders. It was not until she had a near-death experience after eating a large bowl of ice cream that she finally valued the doctor's loving advice.

POINT TO PONDER: *We all have desires, passions, and lusts of our flesh that we want to "freely" enjoy, but when we end up excessively longing for them it becomes sin. These desires can enslave us, as the woman described above, who worshipped ice cream in her heart because it pleased her flesh. Her sinful desire nearly ended her life.*

"Idolatry" is a spiritual problem of our hearts. Most people do not worship little wooden statues as idols, but they are nonetheless idolaters. Idolatry today takes the form of worshiping oneself. It is a violation of the First Commandment in Exodus 20:3: **"You shall have no other**

gods before me." When you are enslaved to any type of "addiction," you are serving the "addiction," which has become your master. That is the definition of idolatry. In the beginning, idolatry and addiction start out as fun and the pleasure serves you. But then at some point your heart desires that idolatrous pleasure so much that your thoughts are consumed by it. You love to chase it and when you obtain it, you are satisfied temporarily, but the consequences are devastating. You could lose everything you ever had materially, and nearly every relationship that had meaning to you. Most of all, you lose yourself: your self-respect, your dignity, and your identity. A submitted relationship with the Lord Christ Jesus is the only solution as you lose yourself in Him, but that's a good loss! Matthew 11:28-30 encourages you: **"Come to me, all who labor and are heavy laden, and I will give you rest. Take my yoke upon you, and learn from me, for I am gentle and lowly in heart, and you will find rest for your souls. For my yoke is easy, and my burden is light."**

PRAYER: "Father, forgive me of my idolatry and sin. Empower me by your Spirit to overcome my addiction that I may find your rest for my soul."

Day 3
REDEFINING "ADDICTION" BIBLICALLY (PART 1)

"But that is not the way you learned Christ!—assuming that you have heard about him and were taught in him, as the truth is in Jesus, to put off your old self, which belongs to your former manner of life and is corrupt through deceitful desires, and to be renewed in the spirit of your minds, and to put on the new self, created after the likeness of God in true righteousness and holiness" (Ephesians 4:20-24).

"I can't help it. I just keep going back to the same old friends. They are the only friends I've got, Mom," yelled Jimmy, after admitting he used an illegal drug. "I have a compulsive disease that I cannot control, Mom, and this disease is incurable, progressive, and fatal. That's what my addictions counselor told me. I can't help it and I will always have it. I will probably always go back to using some kind of drug." Jimmy needs the power of Christ and genuine heart change, but if he continues to call his problem a disease and himself a victim, he will never take full responsibility. He needs to ask God to forgive him, and then allow the Holy Spirit to change and transform him.

POINT TO PONDER: Insanity is often informally defined as "doing the same thing over and expecting different results." Calling an "addiction" a disease keeps people in bondage. Only Christ offers real freedom from "addiction" and the only hope for Jimmy is to view it as a sin nature problem of the will. Until Christ changes his will, Jimmy will always choose some type of addictive pleasure.

If it were up to me, I would always put quotation marks around the word "addiction." Let me explain. "Addiction" is a worldly term and as such defines "addiction" as the "persistent *compulsive* use of a substance known by the user to be harmful."[2] The key word is "compulsive," which implies that one is not responsible for their addictive choices because they cannot help themselves. This is not true because in the early stages of addiction, wrong choices are being made often with a planned purpose to escape from the problems and sorrows of life. A "compulsive" behavior is defined as "an irresistible impulse."[3] But ask yourself: is the choice to fulfill the desire of an addiction in fact *irresistible*? Often the choice is planned. It may *seem* unconscious and unplanned but there is much thinking involved. These words imply that you cannot control your behavior at all, but that is not true or else no one would ever get clean and sober! At some point early in the addiction process, you make a deliberate choice to use your substance of choice at least one time. You are responsible and God holds you responsible for your choices whether you acknowledge Him or not. If you are searching for biblical terms for "addiction" in the Word of God, then study the words "idolatry" and "sin," which describe the problem in general, and "drunkenness" and "sorcery," which describe the problem more specifically.

PRAYER: "Lord, help me to think of my problem of 'addiction' as you do so that I will be transformed and overcome it once and for all."

---

[2] Merriam-Webster, Inc. *Merriam-Webster's Collegiate Dictionary*. Includes index. 10th ed. Springfield, Mass., U.S.A.: Merriam-Webster, 1996, c1993.

[3] Ibid.

Day 4
REDEFINING "ADDICTION" BIBLICALLY (PART 2)

> "Put to death therefore what is earthly in
> you: sexual immorality, impurity, passion,
> evil desire, and covetousness, which is
> idolatry. On account of these the wrath
> of God is coming. In these you too once
> walked, when you were living in them.
> But now you must put them all away:
> anger, wrath, malice, slander, and obscene
> talk from your mouth. Do not lie to one
> another, seeing that you have put off the
> old self with its practices and have put on
> the new self, which is being renewed in
> knowledge after the image of its creator"
> (Colossians 3:4-10).

Teaching a fifteen year old to drive a car is a trying time for any parent! Why? The teenager does not have the experience to drive skillfully because good habits have not yet been established and so it is a slow process. Those who have been driving awhile usually do so without much painstaking effort — seemingly without thinking — because of years of practice and experience.

<u>POINT TO PONDER</u>: *The fact that you can learn bad habits proves that you can learn good habits too. Learn how to replace your bad habits in your thinking, speaking, and acting today with good, biblical habits.*

When you redefine "addiction" as the "persistent *habitual* use of a substance known by the user to be harmful," then "addiction" becomes a word more closely resembling the life-devastating sin of drunkenness described in the

Bible.[4] This new definition of "addiction" also brings more hope to the suffering Christian addict. Because ungodly, destructive habits can be replaced by godly, productive habits, there is hope. Real and lasting change can and will occur in your life.[5] Think about it: if the problem is compulsive, you have no hope of ever overcoming it. However, if the problem is habitual, then you have plenty of power in Christ to replace old thoughts with new thoughts. You can also replace old behaviors with new behaviors that are more Christ-like. You can become that new creation in Christ that 2 Corinthians 5:17 mentions: **"Therefore, if anyone is in Christ, he is a new creation. The old has passed away; behold, the new has come."** Your responsibility is to obey Christ, become more like Him, and make righteous decisions that please God and bring glory to His Name. You can do that with the power of Christ that now dwells within you. That is real hope.

PRAYER: "Father, I want to be nothing like my old, sinful nature in the flesh and desire for you to change me into a new, Spirit-filled creation that looks more like Your Son each and every day."

---

[4] When the word "addiction" is used in the remainder of this book, it will refer to this redefined and new definition since it is biblically more accurate. And the quotation marks will no longer be necessary.

[5] Taken from *The Heart of Addiction*. For a deeper study of "addiction," I recommend you read my other books on that subject as well, since I can only give you a general overview here. www.focuspublishing.com

Day 5
DRUNKENNESS

"And do not get drunk with wine, for that is debauchery, but be filled with the Spirit" (Ephesians 5:18).

Would you drink water from a river that had several thousand gallons of sewage dumped into it? Of course not, because the water is completely contaminated and ruined. The contaminated river can be cleaned up through a gradual filtration and purification process, but it is very expensive. Only then can the water be made useful to the body.

POINT TO PONDER: In a similar way, our physical bodies and minds are contaminated and ruined by sin since we are born with a sinful nature. The Lord must save us and indwell us so that He can "clean" us up through the progressive sanctification process. Our salvation was costly (the sacrifice of Jesus) and the cleansing comes by the Holy Spirit and God's Word. It is a gradual refining process that transforms our polluted being into one that resembles Christ and is useful to the kingdom of God.

Drunkenness is a biblical term that can be applied to the use of any type of mind- or mood-altering drug—not just alcohol. It is a sin to get drunk with wine (or any drug or substance) as it will lead to utter ruin (or "debauchery"). God knows that sin will ruin us by leading us away from Him and into dangerous situations. He discourages our choice to drink wine excessively according to Proverbs 20:1: **"Wine is a mocker, strong drink a brawler, and whoever is led astray by it is not wise."** God wants His best for you and drunkenness is certainly not His best for your life. Sin always destroys relationships and lives. Sin hurts more people than just the sinner. God wants us to be whole and healthy. He wants us to be filled with His Spirit, which is essential for overcoming an addiction of any type. How do we get filled with the Holy Spirit? The answer is in our study of and subsequent obedience to God's Word. The Word of God is mentioned often in conjunction with the Holy Spirit. For example, Ephesians 6:17b refers to **"the sword of the Spirit, which is the word of God."** Also, in Colossians 3:16a, the Bible says: **"Let the word of Christ dwell in you richly..."** The Lord wants our thoughts to be His thoughts so He wants us to replace our thoughts with His Word. The Lord also wants our actions to be like His Son's actions, so we must study the Gospels and all of God's Word to be like Jesus. The Lord wants your will to conform to His will for your life. Refuse to believe the lies of this world and of Satan and replace those lies with God's Word of truth and you will have the power of the Holy Spirit operating in your life.

PRAYER: "Father, reveal to me any lies I am tempted to believe and help me to replace them with your Word of truth."

Day 6
CAN HABITS BE BROKEN?
The Put off / Put on Command

> **"To put off your old self, which belongs to your former manner of life and is corrupt through deceitful desires, and to be renewed in the spirit of your minds, and to put on the new self, created after the likeness of God in true righteousness and holiness"** (Ephesians 4:22-24).

"I'm sorry, Mommy," Billy said as he watched his mother pick up the broken pieces of the pretty teacup he just dropped. Trying to cheer her, he added, "Wait! Don't throw it away. Let me glue the pieces back together." He took the pieces of china and headed to his bedroom. Later, he took his mom to a window and said, "Look out here!" There on the fencepost was the teacup, glued back together and filled with birdseed. The teacup had been transformed into a useful item.

POINT TO PONDER: *Brokenness is God's desire for us when we do not know Him. He wants us to come to the end of ourselves so that we look to Him for new life. Then He can rebuild us into what He wants us to be for His glory and our benefit. Are you a broken teacup that He has restored to newness of life?*

Habits are a good thing. They save us our most valuable resource: time. Good habits are invaluable to a Christian. Bad habits belong to the old self and the sinful nature, but when God places a new heart in us, we are then capable by His power to replace old habits with new habits. One of the most powerful and practical teachings I have learned from the Bible is the put off/put on command which can be applied to any thought, word, or action. God wants us to put off pride and to put on humility. Because humility looks nothing like pride, we will look less like our old self and more like Christ in the lifelong transformation process. Put off harshness and put on gentleness (Ephesians 4:31-32). Put off drunkenness and put on the filling of the Holy Spirit (Ephesians 5:18). Put off stealing and put on working with your own hands and giving to the needy (Ephesians 4:28). Put off bitterness and put on tenderheartedness and forgiveness (Ephesians 4:31-32). The Bible is replete with put-off's and put-on's so that we may become completely transformed into the likeness of Christ, who looks nothing like the harshness, drunkenness, thievery, bitterness, and selfishness that you and I display in our flesh. God does not want to just improve you (also known as recovery), He wants to transform you by making you into something that you never were. Some addicts improve — for example, they are less harsh today than they were yesterday — but God wants them to be gentle today, which looks nothing like harshness. Take this transformation teaching to the next level: you do not have to cope with an addiction for the remainder of your life when you are converted into a new creation, led by and filled with the Holy Spirit of God. Being transformed is what the Lord desires for all of His children, especially those who struggle with any type of addiction. 2 Corinthians 5:17 states: **"Therefore, if anyone is in Christ, he is a new creation. The old has passed away; behold, the new has come."**

PRAYER: "Father, conform my will into yours and transform my image into Your Son's. Make me a new creation and more like Him every day."

Day 7

HOPE OR COPE?

"O Timothy, guard the deposit entrusted to you. Avoid the irreverent babble and contradictions of what is falsely called 'knowledge,' for by professing it some have swerved from the faith" (1 Timothy 6:20-21, quotations mine).

A light switch is not a power source, but it does serve a significant function — that of regulating the flow of electricity into your home. It either allows power to flow through the lines to the light bulb to bring light or it prevents that power from reaching the light bulb.

POINT TO PONDER: You are the light switch. You can either turn the power of Christ on in your life by yielding your will in the flesh to His will in the Spirit. When you live for Him, you will access the power you need to transform your thinking so that your problems do not overwhelm you.

The world offers no hope. The theology of the world can only teach us to "cope" with addiction because it is seen as a lifelong disease with no cure. However, that is not the biblical message of hope. You can certainly be a new creation in Christ through salvation and a spiritual birth. You are dead in your sins until Christ makes you alive in Him and then you begin to spiritually grow as a child of God. Then, as a born again new creation in Christ, God holds His children responsible for their part in the spiritual growth process after salvation. Consider this instruction in Philippians 2:12b-13: **"And now that I am away you must be even more careful to put into action God's saving work in your lives, obeying God with deep reverence and fear. For God is working in you, giving you the desire**

to obey him and the power to do what pleases him." God will do His part to work in you to change your desires and to empower you while you do your part to put your faith into action by reading and obeying the commands in His Word. James 1:22 warns Christians: **"But be doers of the word, and not hearers only, deceiving yourselves."** Please don't misunderstand these commands from the Bible (as some have) who think that this means they earn God's favor and pleasure by working hard at "being good." Nothing could be further from the truth. This process of growing and changing can only occur AFTER God's saving grace has accomplished salvation in your life. Then, after salvation, the power to live a changed life is in the doing of God's Word and not just in the reading or hearing of it. Put God's Word into action in your life today and watch the spiritual blessings flow. The spiritual attacks may increase, but no matter how many temptations you face, God's power working in you will always overcome them.

PRAYER: "Lord, cause me to be a doer of your Word and to put my faith into action today."

Day 8
CALLING SIN "SIN"

> "Let us walk properly as in the daytime, not in orgies and drunkenness, not in sexual immorality and sensuality, not in quarreling and jealousy. But put on the Lord Jesus Christ, and make no provision for the flesh, to gratify its desires" (Romans 13:13-14).

It has been said that employees of banks are trained to study authentic dollar bills so that when they see a counterfeit bill, they can recognize it quickly. They do not have to be able to identify the thousands of various counterfeit currencies floating around because they know so well what the genuine dollar bills looks like. Once we identify the true nature of sin we can learn to recognize it in our behaviors that masquerade as "addictions". Overeating, shopping, gambling, sexual addiction, abuse of drugs and alcohol and countless other addictions are counterfeit terms for what is the genuine problem, and that is sin in our lives.

POINT TO PONDER: Likewise, when you study the Bible to learn God's truth, you will better be able to identify the lies of Satan and this world. Then, you will find true freedom in Christ for the forgiveness of sins.

Sin sounds like an ugly word and it is. In fact, sin is so ugly that God required a real Person to voluntarily give His life to satisfy God's righteous anger for mankind's sin. But the great news is that God Himself provided a Lamb to be slain for the sins of the world in His only begotten Son, the Lord Jesus Christ. Isaiah 53:4-6 tells us that Jesus was sacrificed for our salvation because our sins and "addictions" were placed upon Him: **"Surely he has borne our griefs and carried our sorrows; yet we esteemed him stricken, smitten by God, and afflicted. But he was wounded for our transgressions; he was crushed for our iniquities; upon him was the chastisement that brought us peace, and with his stripes we are healed. All we like sheep have gone astray; we have turned every one to his own way; and the LORD has laid on him the iniquity of us all."** The "he" and the "him" in these verses refer to Jesus Christ. When we see the actions and identify the thoughts accompanying our "addictions" as idolatry and sin, then we have an answer for those sins: the forgiveness of Christ through His shed blood on the Cross. If we call it what the world calls it (a disease) then we no longer have a Savior who heals us from our sins. Christ did not die for the manmade theory of "addiction as a disease" but He died for the sins of idolatry—more specifically drunkenness. Call it "sin" because that is what God calls it to find forgiveness in Christ. 1 John 1:9: **"If we confess our sins, he is faithful and just to forgive us our sins and to cleanse us from all unrighteousness."**

PRAYER: "Father, I confess my sin of idolatry and addiction and ask that you forgive me through the sacrifice of the Lord Jesus Christ. Help me today to walk in newness of life."

Day 9
CONFESSION AND REPENTANCE

> **"Whoever conceals his transgressions will not prosper, but he who confesses and forsakes them will obtain mercy"** (Proverbs 28:13).

"Burying your head in the sand" is a common expression meaning to ignore a problem. But contrary to popular belief, an ostrich does NOT bury its head in the sand. There really is no need to, since an ostrich has strong legs and can run over 40 miles per hour and power kick or peck any dangerous attacker to protect itself.

<u>POINT TO PONDER</u>: *Just as the ostrich has access to amazing power and ability, you have access to God's amazing love and His power to transform your life, but it will first take humility, confession, and repentance.*

Some people mistakenly think it is hurtful to call the actions that accompany addiction "sin," but actually the opposite is true. Calling sin "sin" can bring healing because Christ died for our sins and that brings hope. We find the forgiveness, mercy, and grace of God in confessing and forsaking our sins, but not in hiding, blame-shifting, or concealing our sins. Confession is the first step, which means you are in agreement with God who calls it "sin". Therefore, you must confess it as "sin." The second step is to make your actions agree with your words of confession. Hypocrites are people whose actions do not agree with their words. They say one thing and do another. Many addicts and idolaters are hypocrites and liars. In Proverbs 28:13, God calls us to confess and forsake our transgressions to obtain His mercy. Forsaking sins—also called "repentance"

— is the action part of the confession. Put your faith into action. Not only are you set apart *from* sin, but you are set apart *to* God as a believer in Christ. Real transformation and repentance always includes both the forsaking of the sin and the new behaviors of righteousness to replace those sins. In this way you are to be holy, or set apart, and different from those around you. Being holy simply means "not being ordinary." You serve an extraordinary God who has called you out of the darkness of addiction and into His marvelous light according to 1 Peter 2:9: **"But you are a chosen race, a royal priesthood, a holy nation, a people for his own possession, that you may proclaim the excellencies of him who called you out of darkness into his marvelous light."**

PRAYER: "Father, thank you for making me your possession. Empower me to confess and forsake my sins and transgressions that I might live my life for you today."

Day 10
THE RIGHTEOUSNESS OF CHRIST

"And the LORD God made for Adam and for his wife garments of skins and clothed them" (Genesis 3:21).

A young girl was delighted to find a baby doll near a garbage can in an alley near her home. It was naked and dirty, but she picked it up, took it home, and cleaned it. She and her mother decided to sacrifice one of the girl's own dresses as fabric to sew a hand-made dress for the baby doll. The once naked baby doll is now clothed in the girl's very own garment, sewn especially for the doll.

POINT TO PONDER: *God gave His very own Son to be your sacrifice for sin. Like this doll, you were spiritually naked in sin and the Lord gave His Son to clothe you in a new garment: His righteousness. There was nothing you did to deserve or earn your new clothes. They are given to you by His grace, mercy, and love.*

What I love about the Gospel is this: not only were my sins placed upon Jesus Christ when He was on the cross, but His righteousness was placed upon me. I wear His robe of righteousness before God's eyes now. When Adam and Eve sinned, the Lord made "garments of skins and clothed them" because their own works of fig leaves were insufficient. They needed God's garments of righteousness. Likewise, in Romans 5:17, we are told: **"If, because of one man's trespass, death reigned through that one man, much more will those who receive the abundance of grace and the free gift of righteousness reign in life through the one man Jesus Christ."** The righteousness of Christ is a free gift to us and we should walk in it. No longer do we have to say, "I am an addict" or "I am an alcoholic," because that is not who we are today. We are viewed by God as righteous, but it is not "self-righteousness." It is the righteousness of Christ! Walk in His righteousness today and say, "I am a child of the King. He sees me as righteous." Galatians 4:6-7: **"And because you are sons, God has sent the Spirit of his Son into our hearts, crying, 'Abba! Father!' So you are no longer a slave, but a son, and if a son, then an heir through God."**

PRAYER: "My Abba, Father, thank you for giving me your garment of righteousness and freeing me from my sins. Thank you that I no longer walk in my sins because of your forgiveness offered me through Christ."

Day 11
HURT AND BITTERNESS

"A glad heart makes a happy face; a broken heart crushes the spirit" (Proverbs 15:13).[6]

Marlene had to be rushed from work to the hospital by a co-worker to have emergency surgery to remove her appendix. The physical pain before and after the surgery was excruciating; however, the emotional pain caused by her husband failing to visit her at the hospital was worse, especially when she found out later that he had been seeing another woman and was filing for divorce.

POINT TO PONDER: Marlene's spirit was emotionally and spiritually crushed by her husband's sin against God and against her. No physical pleasure or human being could provide comfort to her soul. Only Christ could heal her spiritual wounds. She found salvation in Him and became forgiving of others, even those who did not "deserve" her forgiveness like her ex-husband. Doesn't that sound just like the Gospel?

One of the most difficult challenges anyone, especially an "addict" faces is how to deal with hurts biblically. Many times, those who turn to addictive pleasure of any type have soft hearts and are hurt easily by others. Sometimes the addict needs to toughen up and not take the hurt so personally. Other times the addict is genuinely hurt by someone else's evil choice and the spiritual wounding of the inner man can be crushing, as mentioned in Proverbs 18:14: **"A man's spirit will endure sickness, but a crushed spirit who can bear?"** Even physical wounds are more easily endured than wounds of the inner spiritual man

[6] *Holy Bible: New Living Translation.* 1997 (Proverbs 15:13). Wheaton, Ill.: Tyndale House.

where emotions are found. Are you broken-hearted today? Who has hurt you? If possible, go to that person and tell him/her of your hurt and your willingness to put the hurt behind you and reconcile your relationship. If the person will not be reconciled or even listen to you right now, then you must do what Jesus did in Luke 23:33-37, which is to *pray* for those who are acting like scoffers, mockers, and enemies: **"And when they came to the place that is called The Skull, there they crucified him, and the criminals, one on his right and one on his left. And Jesus said, 'Father, forgive them, for they know not what they do.' And they cast lots to divide his garments. And the people stood by, watching, but the rulers scoffed at him, saying, 'He saved others; let him save himself, if he is the Christ of God, his Chosen One!' The soldiers also mocked him, coming up and offering him sour wine and saying, 'If you are the King of the Jews, save yourself!'"** Do not allow your hurt to break your spirit, causing bitterness to spring up like a root that grows and spreads to infect you and your loved ones near you. Hebrews 12:15 states: **"See to it that no one fails to obtain the grace of God; that no 'root of bitterness' springs up and causes trouble, and by it many become defiled."** Put off thoughts of bitterness and replace them by putting on thoughts of kindness and tender-heartedness toward others and thoughts of thankfulness toward Christ (Ephesians 4:32).

PRAYER: "Lord, show me how to handle my hurts today. Give me courage to go in humility to those who have hurt me. Help me weed out bitterness so that it does not grow from my hurts. Let me replace sinful thinking with thoughts of who you are, how you love me and what you have done in my life."

Day 12

Forgiveness in a Fallen World

**"Be kind to one another, tenderhearted,
forgiving one another, as God in Christ
forgave you"** (Ephesians 4:32).

*"I love you." Those three little words mean so much to us
when spoken by someone who is important in our lives.
Even more meaningful are the three words, "I forgive you,"
when we have hurt or wronged another person. Imagine
the joyful heart of the man who heard "I forgive you" from
the wife of a man he had accidentally killed in a car wreck.
At that moment he experienced true (agape) love — the
unconditional love of Christ.*

*POINT TO PONDER: "I love you" is a meaningful statement;
however, "I forgive you" is often more significant since it is
a statement of faith in God and it reflects the true, loving
nature of God.*

We live in a fallen, sin-cursed world. Because of Adam's
sin, God pronounced the curse (consequences) upon
mankind (Genesis 3:14-19) and upon God's perfect world.
Even the ground is cursed due to man's sin, as described
in Genesis 3:17b-18: **"cursed is the ground because of
you; in pain you shall eat of it all the days of your life;
thorns and thistles it shall bring forth for you; and you
shall eat the plants of the field."** Think about that for
a moment: the curse of sin affected so much more than
just Adam and Eve. Likewise, your sins of addiction have
harmed others whether you realize it or not. It is likely
that others have hurt you, too. But you don't have to live in
that pain and make it the center of your universe. Instead,
make a list of persons <u>you</u> have hurt and go to them and

ask for their forgiveness. Some may not be willing to give forgiveness right away but God expects you to do your part of humbly confessing your sin, acknowledging the hurt you caused, and asking them, "Will you forgive me?" In a fallen, sin-cursed world, forgiveness is absolutely essential because you will likely hurt others again and they will hurt you. Therefore, you must be forgiving of others just as God in Christ has forgiven you. The only way to overcome God's curse is with God's own power provided by the Holy Spirit. Only His power by His Spirit overcomes the curse that God pronounced on mankind's sin. He alone has the power to transform your life from any addiction that has brought curses to your life.

PRAYER: "Father, thank you for your gift of forgiveness to me. Give me the boldness to ask those I have offended for forgiveness and give me the strength to forgive those who hurt me."

Day 13

TRANSFORMATION (PART 1)

"And we all, with unveiled face, beholding the glory of the Lord, are being transformed into the same image from one degree of glory to another. For this comes from the Lord who is the Spirit" (2 Corinthians 3:18).

One of the most profound mysteries in all of science is the way a caterpillar transforms into a butterfly. This once and for all process, metamorphosis, can be likened to the transformation that occurred in the life of the Apostle Paul, who was transformed like few others in history. A man who formerly killed Christians, Paul was radically transformed by the Person and power of Jesus Christ to become one of the greatest "spokespersons" and proponents of Christianity.

POINT TO PONDER: Only Christ has the power to transform you from a caterpillar (or sinner) into a butterfly (or saint).

"Recovery" is the buzz word in secular addiction counseling. Recovery means "to regain or to recapture one's old self."[7] For physical healing, "recovery" is a good word for it implies an improvement in one's condition. For spiritual healing however, we find a better word in the Bible. Scripture teaches that God desires more for us than "recovery" or that we recapture our old self, because even when we "recover" our old self, we are left with just that—our old self. God desires a total transformation

---

[7] Merriam-Webster, I. 1996, c1993. *Merriam-Webster's Collegiate Dictionary*. Includes index. (10th ed.). Merriam-Webster: Springfield, Mass., U.S.A.

(or conversion).[8] To transform something is to change its "character or condition."[9] Even the word "reform" is inadequate for what God desires to do in an addict's heart because to "reform" something is simply "to change into an improved form or condition."[10] Again, reform is a good word. Reformation is a positive occurrence; but, in the context of addiction, God wants more for the addict. God wants transformation.[11] God wants you to experience His transforming power to make you more like Christ and an entirely new creation. 2 Corinthians 5:17 reminds you: **"Therefore, if anyone is in Christ, he is a new creation. The old has passed away; behold, the new has come."**

PRAYER: "Father, make me a new creation by your transforming power."

---

[8] Taken from *Addiction-Proof Parenting*, chapter 9.
[9] Ibid.
[10] Ibid.
[11] Taken from *Addiction-Proof Parenting*.

Day 14
TRANSFORMATION (PART 2)

> **"Do not be conformed to this world, but
> be transformed by the renewal of your
> mind, that by testing you may discern
> what is the will of God, what is good and
> acceptable and perfect"** (Romans 12:2).

*Little David held his Daddy's hand as they walked along
the beach. The waves crashed onto the shore and suddenly a
large swell overpowered little David and he fell to the sandy
ground, covered by ocean water. Spitting, coughing, and
wiping his face with one hand, he said, "It's good that I'm
holding your hand, Daddy, so that you don't fall, too." His
father laughed, knowing full well the truth that it was HE
who was holding little David's hand.*

POINT TO PONDER: *Sometimes we think we are holding
onto God without His help, but the opposite is true. The
Lord is holding onto us while we cling to Him. He needs no
help from us. We need His power for transformation. We
need to hold onto His Hand by faith, not by sight.*

How does biblical transformation occur? It begins
when someone rejects conforming to the patterned
thinking of this world. In other words, you cannot embrace
worldly terms for what is actually idolatry: addiction,
alcoholism, disease, recovery, and self-help. From the
world's perspective (without a Savior), these terms seem
to appropriately characterize this problem because there
is no hope for lasting change. It is a problem that must be
"coped with" for the rest of one's life by one's *own power*
and self-help. However, for the Christian who believes in
Christ's transforming power, "addiction" is a problem that

can be overcome. It is *not* overcome in your own strength, but in the power of the Holy Spirit working in partnership with God's Word to renew your mind. Your mind (and all of your thinking) must change by becoming more like God's thinking. You want the mind of Christ so that you will be transformed. Therefore, reading, studying, and memorizing passages of Scripture are key components for mind renewal. Colossians 2:8 states: **"See to it that no one takes you captive by philosophy and empty deceit, according to human tradition, according to the elemental spirits of the world, and not according to Christ."** Only when you learn the truth by becoming more biblical in your thinking will you be able to discern the lies of the world that are intended to deceive you.

PRAYER: "Father, renew my mind by the Holy Spirit and Your Word of truth."

Day 15
ANGRY FEELINGS

"Be angry and do not sin; do not let the sun go down on your anger, and give no opportunity to the devil" (Ephesians 4:26-27).

For several weeks Tammy noticed the "check engine" warning light come on every time she drove her car but she ignored it each time. After a month, the car broke down and would not run at all. After it was towed to the mechanic, she was told that a little preventative maintenance when the warning light first appeared would have saved the car, but now it would be best and less costly for her to buy a new vehicle than to have her car repaired.

POINT TO PONDER: Our emotions are warning lights designed to help us to look into our heart to find the real problem. If that problem is ignored, we will eventually break down and possibly be ruined. Confess your sinful anger to God and turn away from the thoughts that caused these emotions in you. Not all emotional responses are sinful but be careful to check your heart's motivation just in case!

Someone in active addiction is often driven by feelings rather than by the commands of God. They are out of control because they are their own final authority. They often hop from one emotional act to another. They submit to no one, acting as though they are god and God does not exist. There is no fear of the Lord in them. Proverbs 1:7 reminds us that **"the fear of the Lord is the beginning of knowledge; fools despise wisdom and instruction."** Emotions are wonderful "smoke alarms," as Lou Priolo so aptly said.[12] What we perceive as our negative emotions

---

[12] Lou Priolo, *Introduction to Biblical Counseling*, a class taught at Eastwood Presbyterian Church, Montgomery, AL, 2002.

often detect the "fires," or the problems, in our lives. When we feel anger, it is an alarm that alerts us to a bigger problem. We become angry when we do not get what we want, which is rooted in our sinful pride and a sense of entitlement. God wants us to learn to think differently than we used to think so that we learn to feel differently than we used to feel. The things that anger you that are selfish, self-centered, or sinful, must be put off and replaced by putting on meekness, or humility, or thinking less of yourself. Trust in the Lord and remember that He is both sovereign and good. What may not seem fair to you may be a trial of your faith. If you fail, you give the devil an opportunity to get his foot in the door of your life. The Lord wants you to wait upon Him and let Him avenge the situation that is causing you to be angry in His way, in His timing, and in His wisdom according to Romans 12:19: **"Beloved, never avenge yourselves, but leave it to the wrath of God, for it is written, 'Vengeance is mine, I will repay, says the Lord.'"**

PRAYER: Pray Psalm 37:8-9 today in a personal way: **"Refrain from anger, and forsake wrath! Fret not yourself; it tends only to evil. For the evildoers shall be cut off, but those who wait for the LORD shall inherit the land."** "Lord, help me to refrain from anger and to forsake my wrath. Help me not to fret (worry) since it leads to evil-doing, which is of the devil. Give me patience to wait upon you so that I might have blessings both in this life and in the life to come in eternity."

Day 16

A HEAVEN-WARD FOCUS

> "Do not love the world or the things in the
> world. If anyone loves the world, the love
> of the Father is not in him. For all that
> is in the world—the desires of the flesh
> and the desires of the eyes and pride in
> possessions—is not from the Father but is
> from the world. And the world is passing
> away along with its desires, but whoever
> does the will of God abides forever" (1
> John 2:15-17).

*A birthright is the privilege of an inheritance simply by
virtue of the wealth of the family to which one is born. In
Genesis 25:29-34, a man named Esau traded his birthright
and all of his inheritance for a bowl of soup. Simply put,
Esau sold his future for a temporary pleasure.*

*POINT TO PONDER: Addicted people plainly choose
temporary pleasures over future promises. It is a focus upon
living for oneself in the moment. It is being overcome by the
desire for a temporary appetite so that one loses sight of
eternity and the future. Do not trade your inheritance from
God for a bowl of soup or any momentary pleasure.*

Where is your focus today? Is it upon the cares of this
world? It is so easy to get focused upon the wrong things.
Temporary things are in the world and are fleeting passions
that never satisfy fully. Addictions of every type take your
focus off the eternal and onto the temporal. God tells us to
obey His will and to be preoccupied with eternal pursuits.
What is eternal in your life today? For some, it is the souls
of your children that are your eternal focus. For others, it

is the souls of co-workers who are lost and headed for an eternal destination of hell. Souls will live forever in one of two places according to Jesus' words in Matthew 25:46: **"And these will go away into eternal punishment, but the righteous into eternal life."** Are you concerned with the souls of others or are you primarily concerned with feeding your own flesh with some type of idolatrous "addiction"? God wants you to intentionally focus on the eternal things. Colossians 3:2-3: **"Set your minds on things that are above, not on things that are on earth. For you have died, and your life is hidden with Christ in God."**

PRAYER: "Father, help me to be intentional by being determined to focus my thoughts on eternity."

Day 17
YOUR NEED FOR CHRIST (PART 1)

> "Therefore, just as sin came into the world through one man, and death through sin, and so death spread to all men because all sinned" (Romans 5:12).

> "Therefore, as one trespass led to condemnation for all men, so one act of righteousness leads to justification and life for all men. For as by the one man's disobedience the many were made sinners, so by the one man's obedience the many will be made righteous" (Romans 5:18-19).

A family in the 1950's received a gift of a black and white television. There was only one problem; it had no antenna and therefore no reception. One day the mother was told that if they connected electronic "rabbit ears" inside the television to an outside antenna, they would be able to see the television programs they wanted. So the family tried it and found it to be true. They were amazed at the transformation of the picture they saw — from only fuzzy snow to crisp pictures.

<u>POINT TO PONDER</u>: *Like this old television, unbelievers need an antenna that provides reception from the Holy Spirit. Someone who is not a Christian does not have the ability to understand the Bible; they are without the power of the Holy Spirit. When someone gets saved, they are "born again" with a new nature of Christ living within and providing powerful "reception" to know God intimately (John 17:3). By the way, "fine tuning" of your life's picture can come from a strong Bible teaching local church.*

Since the sin of Adam in Genesis 3, we live in a fallen world cursed by sin. Some wrongly blame God for death, suffering, selfishness, pain, and sorrow, but the blame is rightly placed upon Adam who was sinfully disobedient. Adam wasn't alone, for Romans 3:23 reminds us, **"for all have sinned and fall short of the glory of God."** Sin can be compared to a term used in the sport of archery. When you take aim, sometimes you simply "miss the mark" or the target that God has set for you. Adam missed the mark and as a result of his sin, everyone is born with a sinful nature. Our hearts are as bent toward sin like a bicycle wheel that has hit a curb and become crooked. That wheel awkwardly rolls toward the direction of its crookedness. Likewise, your bent is to fulfill the desires of your heart — to satisfy the temporary passions of your flesh. For this reason, you need a new nature and a new heart that is given by the indwelling of the Holy Spirit.

PRAYER: "Father, I confess that my sinful heart is prone to wander far from you. **Create in me a clean heart, O God, and renew a right spirit within me"** (Psalm 51:10).

Day 18

YOUR NEED FOR CHRIST (PART 2)

> "Create in me a clean heart, O God, and
> renew a right spirit within me" (Psalm 51:10).

"Lord, take away my desire for chocolate donuts," Terry prayed as he stared at the plate of donuts at a reception party. Soon after his prayer, he walked over to the dessert table to look at the donuts more closely. He continued to pray, "Lord, please take away my desire for these donuts!" Minutes later, a friend observed Terry eating a donut at his table. "I thought you were on a diet," he said. Terry justified his actions by telling the friend, "God never took away my desire for this donut so I am going to enjoy it."

*POINT TO PONDER: How many times do we pray for God to act, but we fail to do our part! The Christian life consists of prayer but it also consists of action according to 1 Corinthians 4:20: "**For the kingdom of God does not consist in talk but in power.**" If you have a new nature within you, then you must constantly say "no" to your will in the flesh and say "yes" to God's will in the Spirit just as Jesus did in Luke 22:42. Do pray but also do your part to be obedient and responsible to Christ. Stop staring at what you cannot have and focus on what you can have.*

We are born with a sinful nature and so we are destined to wrestle with that sin nature our entire lives. But with the promise of God's Spirit indwelling us, we have the power we need for the battle. Just as the Lord promised the Israelites in Ezekiel 36:25-27, you can ask God to powerfully change your life: **"I will sprinkle clean water on you, and you shall be clean from all your uncleannesses, and from all your idols I will cleanse you. And I will give you a** new heart, and a new spirit I will put within you. And I will remove the heart of stone from your flesh and give you a heart of flesh. And I will put my Spirit within you, and cause you to walk in my statutes and be careful to obey my rules." Christians have a new life in Christ but they must still battle the old habit patterns of their flesh. The Apostle Paul tells us how to win our war against the flesh in Galatians 5:16-18: "But I say, walk by the Spirit, and you will not gratify the desires of the flesh. For the desires of the flesh are against the Spirit, and the desires of the Spirit are against the flesh, for these are opposed to each other, to keep you from doing the things you want to do. But if you are led by the Spirit, you are not under the law." God gives you His Holy Spirit to live inside you to guide, teach, and empower you to overcome any addiction. 2 Timothy 1:14 says: "By the Holy Spirit who dwells within us, guard the good deposit entrusted to you." When you become frustrated by your fleshly desires and wonder why God isn't helping you resist, ask yourself if you are doing your part. As you study the Scriptures, the Holy Spirit will work in you to renew your mind and to accomplish God's will through you according to Philippians 2:13: "for it is God who works in you, both to will and to work for his good pleasure."

PRAYER: "Father God, I want your Spirit to dominate me so that I accomplish your plan, your will, and your purposes and not my own."

Day 19

THE POWER OF CHRIST IN YOU!

> **"For it is God who works in you, both to will and to work for his good pleasure"** (Philippians 2:13).

Billy and his dad were practicing baseball. Billy really wanted to hit home runs. "The proper swing of the bat provides the power you need to hit a home run, Billy," said his Dad, pulling him aside from home plate for a minute. "And don't 'overswing' at the ball." Billy had had the wrong goal. All Billy wanted was a home run; he was swinging with everything he had, never getting close to achieving his goal. After this instructional talk with Dad, Billy's goal changed. He only wanted to swing under control to make good contact with the ball. Billy stepped up to the plate for the final 10 minutes of batting practice. Dad pitched the ball, and Billy swung the bat just as his Dad had instructed — under control. He went from zero home runs during the first 20 minutes, to hitting two home runs in the final 10 minutes.

POINT TO PONDER: You do not need to "help God out" by accomplishing your goals and your will. Instead, conform your goals to His goals and do what He tells you to do as an act of faith. The results—whether good or bad—are up to Him, are all for His glory and for your good.

There is no such thing as "willpower" for an addict or idolater. However, there is such a thing as the "will of God power" as the Holy Spirit works in believers to change our will and to empower us to carry out God's will. Before the foundation of the world, God had plans for us according to Ephesians 2:10: **"For we are his workmanship, created in Christ Jesus for good works, which God prepared**

beforehand, that we should walk in them." It is amazing love to think that God prepared good works for us to work out in our lives even though we once led the life of a selfish, idolatrous, and addicted person. God's redeeming love is powerful and life-changing. Now, as someone who still has a will, you must daily, and sometimes hourly, be accepting and trusting of the Father's will, just as Jesus did in Luke 22:42 when He prayed, **"Father, if you are willing, remove this cup from me. Nevertheless, not my will, but yours, be done."** If Jesus had to submit His will as a man unto the Father's will, then it is even more vital that you do the same to overcome your addiction. Do not be ruled by your feelings but be ruled by the will of God which is to obey His commands. Then, you will find the blessings both in this life and in the life to come.

PRAYER: "Lord God, help me to know that your will is best for me and that I must constantly say, 'Not my will, but your divine will be done in my life today.'"

Day 20
Becoming Spiritually Mature and Strong

"For the word of the cross is folly to those who are perishing, but to us who are being saved it is the power of God" (1 Corinthians 1:18).

After school one day the custodian watched a young teen alone in the gym preparing to work out. "What are you doing, young man?" he asked. The boy explained that he really wanted to make the high school football team in the fall and he knew he must get into shape over the summer. After a few minutes of conversation, the custodian realized the boy had no idea how to strengthen his body effectively and safely. He kindly offered to train the boy twice each week. They worked together and by the end of the summer, the results were noticeable in the young man's body as he physically matured.

POINT TO PONDER: *You may have goals that you want to achieve, but you need someone else to come alongside you to encourage, plan, push, challenge, and instruct you in your spiritual life, especially in regard to overcoming an addiction.*

It is the seemingly "foolish" message of the cross that saves you and the same power that saves you is the power that spiritually grows you. To overcome your addiction, you must grow in Christ. You cannot stay a babe in Christ because you will likely fall prey to the temptations of Satan, this world, and your flesh. Hebrews 5:12-14 emphasizes the need for spiritual growth to discern good from evil: **"For though by this time you ought to be teachers, you need someone to teach you again the basic principles**

of the oracles of God. You need milk, not solid food, for everyone who lives on milk is unskilled in the word of righteousness, since he is a child. But solid food is for the mature, for those who have their powers of discernment trained by constant practice to distinguish good from evil." Solid spiritual food is found in learning and applying the Word of God. If you are still a babe in Christ you need a trusted Christian friend to mentor and disciple you. The Christian walk was never meant to be alone. You need Christ and those who are mature in Christ to walk with you as you overcome your addiction. Find a mentor, trusted Christian friend, or church leader to disciple you today.

PRAYER: "Father, please send me a mature believer in Christ to disciple and mentor me so that I may continue to grow, and then be able to disciple others who need encouragement for overcoming their addictions."

Day 21
FEAR

"There is no fear in love, but perfect love casts out fear. For fear has to do with punishment, and whoever fears has not been perfected in love. We love because [he first loved us" (1 John 4:18-19).

"I can't do it. I hate spiders!" exclaimed a mother to her husband on the phone. Startled by a spider, she was paralyzed by fear as she stopped preparing lunch for her 10 month old daughter. Not knowing what to do, she stared at the "giant" spider on the floor hoping it would not come toward her. Unaware of her child's whereabouts, the baby crawled through her legs toward the spider to attempt to grab it. "Noooo!" she bellowed out as the child got within reach of the spider. The mother suddenly darted over, stepped on the spider, and crushed it.

<u>POINT TO PONDER</u>: *Thinking of others ahead of yourself is a key to overcoming any unrighteous fear. Think of Christ first and be obedient to Him regardless of your fears and He will make a way in your life to carry on beyond your fears.*

Fear is a powerful emotion with potential for good or evil. Righteous fear protects you from harm. It is good to fear poisonous snakes so that you do not play with them and risk a venomous bite that may kill you. On the other hand, sinful fear may keep you from doing the will of God by faith. Fear is equivalent to doubt and not trusting Christ. For example, you may have an overwhelming fear of snakes and because you once saw one in a neighbor's yard you have vowed to never set foot in that yard again. What will you do if the neighbor calls you in an emergency and asks you to come help them? You must then allow perfect love—God's love—to empower you to overcome your feelings of fear, to help the neighbor, and to obey the Lord. God wants you to trust in Him and not be crippled by overwhelming fear.

Many addicts fear what others think, obsessing about what others think of them rather than what Christ thinks of them. They are crippled by fear and are people-pleasers according to Galatians 1:10: **"For am I now seeking the approval of man, or of God? Or am I trying to please man? If I were still trying to please man, I would not be a servant of Christ."** The only force more powerful than fear is God's perfect love which casts out fear (1 John 4:18). Human love is often conditional and performance-based, and it often dictates your people-pleasing tendencies. However, God's love is unconditional and not based upon our performance since **"we love because he first loved us."** In other words, God first loved you while you were unloving toward Him according to Romans 5:8: **"but God shows his love for us in that while we were still sinners, Christ died for us."** This love is called "agape" love—it has nothing to do with our performance. Embrace God's love for you today and do not be overwhelmed by fear or any of your other emotions. Instead, live by faith in obedience to God's Word and not according to your own feelings: **"Trust in the LORD with all your heart, and do not lean on your own understanding"** (Proverbs 3:5).

PRAYER: "Father, thank you for your agape love for me that is unconditional and is provided through the righteousness of Christ. Enable me to embrace your perfect love for me today so that all of my unrighteous fears will be overcome by the power of the Holy Spirit."

Day 22
DOING WHAT IS RIGHT

"Everyone then who hears these words of mine and does them will be like a wise man who built his house on the rock. And the rain fell, and the floods came, and the winds blew and beat on that house, but it did not fall, because it had been founded on the rock. And everyone who hears these words of mine and does not do them will be like a foolish man who built his house on the sand. And the rain fell, and the floods came, and the winds blew and beat against that house, and it fell, and great was the fall of it" (Matthew 7:24-27).

"I'll get to it later," calls the husband to his wife as he watches television. His wife just reminded him about fixing the leaky faucet in their kitchen. He forgets about it again and several weeks later the bottom shelf in the cabinet has gotten so wet that it is rotted. Now, he must fix both the faucet and the cabinet shelf. His wife said, "I asked you to fix it earlier and you didn't so now you've got to do twice as much work." The husband answers, "I know ... I wanted to do it. I just never got around to it."

POINT TO PONDER: Mankind is called to be a "doer" of the Word and not just a "hearer" only (James 1:22). Saying you'll do it but not doing it is not good enough. Good intentions without following through with actions will not help you to overcome your addiction. God calls us to be obedient to His Word in our thoughts, words, and actions.

The last thing Jesus said as He preached His well-known Sermon on the Mount in Matthew 7 emphasized the doing of His teachings. In other words, Jesus was saying to His followers, "Now that you have heard My Words, do My Words by putting them into action. Go and love God and others." In the closing of this sermon, Jesus compared two men: one wise, one foolish. Both men heard the Word of Christ. Both men built houses. Both men experienced trials and the storms of life. However, there was one key difference between the two men: action. The wise man put the words of Christ into action in his life and was a doer. The fool only heard the words and failed to do them.[13] When the problems of life came his way, the fool's house was destroyed. Psalm 14:1 says: **"The fool says in his heart. 'There is no God.' They are corrupt, they do abominable deeds, there is none who does good."** Fools are *not* stupid. They are very smart. Fools are simply rebellious toward the Lord. Addicts act like fools who conveniently "forget" there is a God to whom they are accountable. Today, live your life in light of God's mercy and in an awareness of His presence all day long.

PRAYER: "Father, help me to remember that you know all about me including my thoughts, emotions, and desires. Remind me that you see all that I do and that you love me."

---

[13] I am thankful to Randy Patten, current president of NANC, for this sound teaching on Matthew 7, that he gives in a DVD biblical counseling observations course available at www.fbclafayette.org

Day 23
HUMILITY

> "Have this mind among yourselves, which is yours in Christ Jesus, who though he was in the form of God, did not count equality with God a thing to be grasped, but made himself nothing, taking the form of a servant, being born in the likeness of men. And being found in human form, he humbled himself by becoming obedient to the point of death, even death on a cross" (Philippians 2:5-8).

Freddie is a star college athlete who has potential to play professional ball but he never learned how to read. In high school, his coaches and teachers passed him in all of his classes because of his tremendous athletic ability and his charismatic personality. Now in college, Freddie mistakenly thinks that he can get by with minimal effort because he has for his entire life, and after all, he's good enough to go pro after a couple of years anyway. Sadly, Freddie flunks out after the first semester, and never makes it to the pros. Freddie learned to put forth minimal effort all throughout his life. Sadly, the people who supposedly cared about him lied for him and allowed him to pass. Freddie had developed an entitlement mentality (I deserve to play professionally) and failed to work hard in learning to read when he was very young all the way through college.

POINT TO PONDER: Learn from Freddie and fight the entitlement mentality and the pride that accompanies it. Learn to be humble, teachable, and hungry to know God.

Many addicts have what I call an "entitlement" mentality. They believe they deserve better and are entitled to certain things. When in active addiction, they fail to have the mind of Christ, which is to be humble. Christ, though He is a King, came to serve us. Matthew 20:26b-28 teaches us about servant-leadership and humility through the teachings of Jesus: **"But whoever would be great among you must be your servant, and whoever would be first among you must be your slave, even as the Son of Man came not to be served but to serve, and to give his life as a ransom for many."** If anyone should have righteously felt "entitled" to certain rights, it was Jesus Christ; yet He did not come to be served but to serve us. His sacrificial leadership was a perfect display of servant-hood and knowing that should amaze and humble you. Therefore, the next time you feel "entitled" to something better in this life; just remember the example of Jesus in Philippians 2 and in Matthew 20. Fight to keep humility in the center of your mind rather than passively allowing the prideful thoughts (that you are entitled to a better life) to creep into your mind. Proverbs 11:2 says: **"When pride comes, then comes disgrace, but with the humble is wisdom."** [14]

PRAYER: "Father, keep in the forefront of my mind your display of humility so that I might not become prideful and boast in my own accomplishments."

---

[14] For a deeper study on pride and humility, I highly recommend a small booklet written by Dr. Stuart Scott called "From Pride to Humility" available through Focus Publishing: www.focuspublishing.com.

Day 24
HELPING OTHERS IS THE HEART OF GOD

"In all things I have shown you that by working hard in this way we must help the weak and remember the words of the Lord Jesus, how he himself said, 'It is more blessed to give than to receive'" (Acts 20:35).

Stacy ordered two of the same books from an online discount store for a class she was taking with a friend. When the books arrived, Stacy noticed that one of them was in poor condition while the other was in excellent condition. Stacy decided to give the best one to her friend and to keep the poor one for herself so that God would be glorified as she demonstrated to her friend the love of God.

POINT TO PONDER: Stacy knew the heart of God was for her to be a giver rather than a taker so she gave the best book to her friend. Her friend noticed the sacrifice and thanked Stacy for her thoughtfulness. Their friendship was strengthened as a result of this one simple exchange.

Giving is the heart of God as seen visibly in John 3:16: **"For God so loved the world, that He gave His only Son."** God gives and **"God is love"** (1 John 4:8b). What can you give to God that He does not already have? All He wants from you is worship. That is one reason why addiction is a "worship disorder" of idolatry. The addict is worshiping the wrong person: himself! God wants your whole life to consist of actions that worship Him according to 1 Corinthians 10:31: **"So, whether you eat or drink, or whatever you do, do all to the glory of God."** Everything we do is either in faith unto God or in weakness or selfishness unto our self. We either seek to please God or seek to please self. There are simply two roads of glory: one road is to walk and live for the glory of God and the other is to walk and live for the glory of self. God wants us to give to others. When we help others, we are demonstrating the heart of God and we are glorifying Him. That is one reason why stealing is so sinfully harmful. Stealing is taking and God is a Giver. Stealing hurts others and it does not reflect the generous, gracious, and giving character of God. Find ways today to give and to help others and you will be an ambassador of Christ (2 Corinthians 5:20).

PRAYER: "Father, make my heart like yours by providing me with opportunities to give of my time, talents, and treasures to others."

Day 25
ALCOHOL IS A DRUG

"Give strong drink to the one who is perishing, and wine to those in bitter distress" (Proverbs 31:6).

Cheryl's friend, Elizabeth, is dying of cancer and in extreme physical pain daily. She takes pain medication to help her feel some relief from her bitter distress. Cheryl, on the other hand, feels as if she is living in extreme emotional pain because of the circumstances in her life: her boyfriend broke up with her, her dog recently died, her parents do not trust her, her job is difficult and unfulfilling, and she is thousands of dollars in debt due to frivolous spending. To Cheryl, her "pain" is excruciating and similar to her friend's physical pain from cancer, so Cheryl takes pain medications to escape from the harsh realities of her life. Sadly, the circumstances in her life only become worse.

<u>POINT TO PONDER</u>: *Taking any drug, alcohol included, for reasons other than physical pain may seem justified in a person's mind, but there is no justification for irresponsible and selfish illicit drug use.*

Unfortunately, people have been brainwashed by the world's language and teaching to think of alcohol as something different from drugs. This is the world's differentiation; the Bible makes no distinction. For this reason, when you read of "drunkenness" in the Bible, it can be applied to the effect that drugs have on the body since alcohol is just one of many drugs available to us. Yes, let me say it again, alcohol is a drug in a liquid form just as cough syrup with codeine is a drug in liquid form. Does the liquidity of it make it any less a drug? "In reality, alcohol is a drug just like marijuana, cocaine, opiates, benzodiazepine, methamphetamine, nicotine, and even caffeine. God in His Word describes your drug problem (or drinking to excess) as 'drunkenness,' whether it is alcohol or any other drug, legal or illegal, that you are using to get high or low."[15] Whether you drink it, shoot it, snort it, smoke it, or inhale it, a drug is a drug. In other words, the method of intake makes no difference. The use of drugs to excess without a solid medical reason is sin. In one moment of time, a choice is made to obey a desire of your heart (lusts of the flesh) rather than deny yourself and do the will of God. Every individual is responsible for those choices to pursue pleasing self rather than God and others. Those choices are acts of the will. The more a person chooses to give in to a temporary satisfaction that never completely fulfills the heart, the more a person becomes "addicted," which most recognize as a life that is "out of control."

Remember, God looks at your heart's motives for why you are using any drug. 1 Samuel 16:7 reminds us that God's criteria for evaluating someone is the heart: **"But the LORD said to Samuel, 'Do not look on his appearance or on the height of his stature, because I have rejected him. For the LORD sees not as man sees: man looks on the outward appearance, but the LORD looks on the heart.'"**

PRAYER: "Lord, thank you that you see into my heart and judge my motives. Help me to use your Word by the power of the Holy Spirit to analyze my own heart biblically so that I might grow in Christ."

---

[15] Shaw, Mark, *The Heart of Addiction*, Focus Publishing: Bemidji, MN.

Day 26
A PICTURE OF DRUNKENNESS

> "Who has woe? Who has sorrow? Who has strife? Who has complaining? Who has wounds without cause? Who has redness of eyes? Those who tarry long over wine; those who go to try mixed wine. Do not look at wine when it is red, when it sparkles in the cup and goes down smoothly. In the end it bites like a serpent and stings like an adder. Your eyes will see strange things, and your heart utter perverse things. You will be like one who lies down in the midst of the sea, like one who lies on the top of a mast. 'They struck me,' you will say, 'but I was not hurt; they beat me, but I did not feel it. When shall I awake? I must have another drink'" (Proverbs 23:29-35).

Little fifteen-month old Matthew kept trying to put a square block into a round hole on his play toy. The round block went right in so Matthew just assumed the square one would also. Matthew tries to put the square through the round hole for five minutes and then cries out loud in frustration and throws the square block. All the while, the square hole was within his reach.

POINT TO PONDER: How much like Matthew are we? We try to do the same things over and over and expect different results. An addiction involves choosing the same addictive pleasure over and over yet thinking the outcome will bring satisfaction "this time." Do not fool yourself: a choice for an addiction will produce the same miserable outcome each and every time.

There is not a clearer picture of drunkenness in Scripture than the lesson in Proverbs 23:29-35 above. It begins with a series of questions that are only answered by "a drunkard." A drunkard is hopeless and his only temporary hope exists in watching the alcohol sparkle in the cup knowing it will go down smoothly. The Bible never says that sin won't look and feel good. It does. That's why it is tempting. It appeals to our flesh. Sadly, the reality of drunkenness is that it strikes the drunkard in the end like a venomous snake. The heart utters perverse things and there are physical consequences, too. The picture is that of a fool who in the end only wants to come out of his drunken stupor so that he might drink again. Do not get caught in this cyclical trap of your flesh. Instead, say "no" to alcohol, drugs, and any addiction and say "yes" to living a righteous, pleasant, and pleasing life unto God. You have much to look forward to in your new life in Christ. God wants you to be a drunkard no longer, but to have a new identity—a Spirit-filled believer in Christ (Ephesians 5:18). That is the transforming power of Christ.

PRAYER: "Lord, thank you that I am no longer caught in the snare of addiction and drunkenness and that you are leading me by your Spirit to have an abundant life now and in eternity."

Day 27
THE LORD EXAMINES THE HEART

> "For the word of God is living and active,
> sharper than any two-edged sword,
> piercing to the division of soul and of
> spirit, of joints and of marrow, and
> discerning the thoughts and intentions of
> the heart. And no creature is hidden from
> his sight, but all are naked and exposed
> to the eyes of him to whom we must give
> account" (Hebrews 4:12-13).

A young boy named David was anointed king of the Jews by a prophet named Samuel. God led Samuel to choose David because God knew David's heart. Scripture says that David was a man after God's own heart. Interestingly, when Samuel came to the house of Jesse, David's father, he asked to meet all of his sons, but David was not invited to the gathering because his father considered the outward boyish appearance of David—he did not look like a king.

POINT TO PONDER: God's thoughts are different than mankind's thoughts because God looks at our hearts. God knows our hearts must be transformed from hearts that choose to please self into hearts that choose to please God. When your heart is right, God will choose you to do great things for His spiritual kingdom.

The Bible is a spiritual book. It can only be correctly understood by the illuminating power of the Holy Spirit. We must pray before we read it and ask the Lord to open our eyes by His Spirit. Then, the Bible will be a living and active book that will reveal the condition of our heart to us. God already knows our heart. Jeremiah 17:9 reminds us that

"**The heart is deceitful above all things, and desperately sick; who can understand it? I the LORD search the heart and test the mind, to give every man according to his ways, according to the fruit of his deeds.**" Only God can search the heart which contains our thoughts, motives, desires, passions, attitudes, and emotions. God holds us accountable for our thoughts, too, according to what Jesus taught in Matthew 5:28: "**But I say to you that everyone who looks at a woman with lustful intent has already committed adultery with her in his heart.**" It can be scary to realize that God examines our motives and our thoughts. We need to confess our thoughts to Him and ask for His forgiveness. Then, we need to replace those selfish thoughts with godly thoughts of righteousness that come from His Word. Remember that His Word will help you to become more godly and Christ-like as Isaiah 55:8-9 reminds us: "**For my thoughts are not your thoughts, neither are your ways my ways, declares the LORD. For as the heavens are higher than the earth, so are my ways higher than your ways and my thoughts than your thoughts.**"

PRAYER: "Father, I need your thoughts today to replace my faulty, selfish thinking. Renew my mind today by your Spirit and with your Word of truth."

Day 28
SHARING GOD'S COMFORT WITH OTHERS

> "Blessed be the God and Father of our Lord Jesus Christ, the Father of mercies and God of all comfort, who comforts us in all our affliction, so that we may be able to comfort those who are in any affliction, with the comfort with which we ourselves are comforted by God" (2 Corinthians 1:3-4).

Billy and his wife experienced the nearly fatal drowning of their son. God saved the child's life even though he was underwater for almost two minutes. Billy wondered why God allowed them to go through that until he met a couple the very next week who were visiting his church. It all became clear to him when they shared with him the loss of their child. Billy immediately had compassion for this couple when he heard their story because of what he had experienced the prior week.

POINT TO PONDER: Share the comfort, hope, grace, kindness, and love you have experienced from the Lord with others.

So often our difficult experiences are preparing us to have compassion and understanding with others in similar situations. Did you ever consider that maybe one reason God allowed you to sin and get caught in the snare of addiction is that you might help others? With the same comfort you have received from Christ, so are you now to comfort others. People need the life-giving message that any addiction can be overcome and that we can be transformed by the power of Christ. Your testimony is a powerful witness to others as it gives glory to Him and you should share it when led by Him to do so. You never know the impact your testimony might have on others who need to see Christ in you. He is the hope of glory. 1 Peter 1:3-5 states: **"Blessed be the God and Father of our Lord Jesus Christ! According to his great mercy, he has caused us to be born again to a living hope through the resurrection of Jesus Christ from the dead, to an inheritance that is imperishable, undefiled, and unfading, kept in heaven for you, who by God's power are being guarded through faith for a salvation ready to be revealed in the last time."** Share your faith in Christ with someone today to bring encouragement to them and hope in Christ. Live in such a way that you show forth the praises of the One who has called you out of darkness and into His marvelous light.

PRAYER: "Father, show me how and where and with whom I can share my faith today so that they might receive the same comfort you have given me in Christ Jesus."

Day 29
Giving and Not Consuming

> **"And he said to him, "You shall love the Lord your God with all your heart and with all your soul and with all your mind. This is the great and first commandment. And a second is like it: You shall love your neighbor as yourself. On these two commandments depend all the Law and the Prophets"** (Matthew 22:37-40).

Alison received ten dollars for her tenth birthday and her mother said she could spend it on anything she wanted, so she did. She bought candy and little trinket toys for herself that broke soon after she played with them. The candy and toys were gone in just two days. At church the next Sunday, the pastor mentioned a needy family who lost everything they owned in a fire. Alison wanted to give money to help this family since she knew the children personally but she did not have any money left to give.

POINT TO PONDER: Alison learned a very valuable lesson about saving money and giving to those in real need rather than spending money on the first temporary, selfish pleasures that she sees.

One of the mentalities of persons caught in active addiction is the "consumer" mentality. In *Addiction-Proof Parenting*, a consumer is defined as "someone who destroys, spends wastefully, squanders, and uses up things."[16] To consume a product is to use it fully. A fire that consumes a house burns it completely down to the ground. A child

---

[16] Shaw, Mark, *Addiction Proof Parenting*, Focus Publishing: Bemidji, MN.

who is a consumer uses everything to its fullest extent, including people! Those who possess a consumer mentality do not think with a grateful heart. Their desire is to spend all of their possessions upon their own selfish pursuits rather than helping others. This consumer mentality is based upon a failure to follow the second part of the Great Commandment in Matthew 22:39: **"And a second is like it: You shall love your neighbor as yourself."** The neighbor in this verse means "near one." Sometimes when we read that verse we think of a next door neighbor who lives beside us. However, a neighbor is best understood to be someone who is near us in our everyday life. Examples of near ones include family members, colleagues at work, other students at school, friends, and people you see regularly at the grocery store. So, how should you love your near ones? One way is by giving of your time, talents, and treasures to help someone in need. Being a blessing to others is a crucial component of the committed Christian walk. However, the consumer is primarily concerned with pleasing one person: self. Therefore, their time, talents, and treasures are wrongly spent for selfish pursuits without consideration of others. For example, money may be spent on an "addictive" shopping spree for enjoyment rather than on the electric bill.[17] Be a giver (and not a consumer) for the glory of God today.

PRAYER: "Father, mold me into a giver and help me to use the gifts you have given to me for the benefit of others and to glorify you."

---

[17] Taken from *Addiction-Proof Parenting*. Also, please understand the word "addictive" to describe a shopping spree is a worldly idea and the Bible would describe it as being a poor steward of God-given resources or idolatry.

Day 30

RESPONSIBILITY

> "<u>And do not get drunk with wine, for
> that is debauchery, but be filled with the
> Spirit</u>, addressing one another in psalms
> and hymns and spiritual songs, singing
> and making melody to the Lord with all
> your heart, giving thanks always and for
> everything to God the Father in the name
> of our Lord Jesus Christ, submitting to
> one another out of reverence for Christ"
> (Ephesians 5:18-21, emphasis mine).

*Liz has a long history of changing jobs. The reason is always
the same: conflict with her supervisors or boss. She has never
learned to submit to her authorities. In fact, she has always
lived for herself and often says: "I do what I want to do." Sadly,
Liz's parents continue to help her to remain irresponsible
by taking her side and financially supporting her when she
quits a new job. They never allow Liz to experience any
negative consequences after she quits a job so she continues
to make poor decisions.*

*POINT TO PONDER: Negative consequences can mean that
the Lord is teaching you a valuable lesson by disciplining
you to make you more obedient and responsible like Christ
(Romans 8:29). God disciplines His children that He loves
(Hebrews 12:3-17).*

Many addicts struggle in the area of responsibility.
Some see themselves as victims and have a "victim
mentality." "A victim mentality is defined as the belief that
one has been wronged by another person which develops
into an outlook on life that is self-defeating. They feel

powerless though they are not. Sometimes the offense is real. There are true victims in this world. When a child is hurt by parents, he or she may wrongly turn to drugs or some other form of idolatry to escape, cope, and deal with the pain. This choice is not God's best for the child and will only lead to further problems.[18] A victim mentality is a detrimental way of thinking that leads you away from responsibility and obedience to Christ because you falsely believe you are powerless. Blame-shifting is commonly seen and heard from false "victims" who think nothing is their own fault. Ephesians 5:18 gives the addict a key step in overcoming drunkenness, idolatry, or addiction: take responsibility for your actions by being filled with the Holy Spirit. A Spirit-filled life is an obedient and responsible life that glorifies God and loves others. It is not emotionally driven but obedience driven. Real power is realizing that God holds you responsible to those things in your control and that you are to yield your will to His will. When you understand that He is sovereign and you are responsible, you will overcome your addiction successfully.

PRAYER: "Lord, lead me to understand my responsibilities and not to shift blame or give in to victim thinking today."

---

[18] Taken from *Addiction-Proof Parenting*.

Day 31

GRATITUDE

> "And do not get drunk with wine, for that is debauchery, but be filled with the Spirit, <u>addressing one another in psalms and hymns and spiritual songs, singing and making melody to the Lord with all your heart</u>, giving thanks always and for everything to God the Father in the name of our Lord Jesus Christ, submitting to one another out of reverence for Christ" (Ephesians 5:18-21, emphasis mine).

"I can't buy those tickets," Marvin exclaimed. "The computer locked up again because it is a piece of junk!" Marvin's wife calmly replied, "Marvin, maybe God doesn't want you to buy them right now. Maybe He is hindering you. Why don't you go to bed now, pray and ask God's forgiveness for your impatience, and try again in the morning?" Marvin grumbled under his breath and went to bed and prayed. As soon as he was able to go to his computer the next day, Marvin tried again to buy the tickets, but before he purchased them the phone rang. It was a friend who had two free tickets to give Marvin to the very same event!

<u>*POINT TO PONDER:*</u> *God knows the future and He knew Marvin's friend would call at just that exact time with good news that he was giving the tickets away. God wants us to see His sovereign, loving Hand in all events of our lives even when we do not fully understand all of His plans for us.*

Those active in addiction tend to have a "perishing mentality." Proverbs 31:6-7 instructs us to: **"Give strong drink to the one who is perishing, and wine to those in**

bitter distress; let them drink and forget their poverty and remember their misery no more." Someone in active addiction thinks they are dying, or perishing, as they are often living in complete bitterness. Their own hurts and wounds are eating them alive spiritually through anger, hopelessness, and bitterness. They desperately turn to an addiction to escape the pain and flee to pleasure even if it is temporary and fleeting. Who is it that you are bitter towards today? Do you need to forgive that person in your heart and/or do you need to ask the person for forgiveness? Either way, a perishing mentality is a detrimental way to live because the person in this mindset thinks "woe is me" and focuses too much on self. These hurts become the center of one's universe and it leads to self-pity and pride. The antidote for this destructive mentality is found in Ephesians 5:19-20 above: gratitude. Let your words addressed to others be like music to their ears. Bitter persons defile many people, according to Hebrews 12:15, so people will pick up on your bitterness. It will not be hidden from them. Therefore, focus your mind on being joyful today. A joyful mentality is only produced as a fruit of the Holy Spirit (Galatians 5:22-23) and it is an intentional mindset that is not swayed by one's circumstances. Give thanks to God always for everything in the name of our Lord Jesus Christ. Be grateful today for all He has done for you and focus upon His goodness and not your perishing mentality.

PRAYER: "God, help me to focus upon your grace to me that I might be thankful and be a delight to others. I want to reflect your goodness today."

Day 32
SUBMISSION

> "And do not get drunk with wine, for that is debauchery, but be filled with the Spirit, addressing one another in psalms and hymns and spiritual songs, singing and making melody to the Lord with all your heart, <u>giving thanks always and for everything to God the Father in the name of our Lord Jesus Christ, submitting to one another out of reverence for Christ</u>" (Ephesians 5:18-21, emphasis mine).

A simple game of "follow the leader" breaks down as soon as one of followers decides to go his own way apart from the leader. Confusion ensues as the followers behind the rebellious follower of the leader are torn between following the real leader or the rebel.

<u>POINT TO PONDER</u>: *Simple submission to the Leader, Christ, leads to peace, protection, and blessings.*

While in active addiction, many addicts have a "rebellious" mentality. Someone who is rebellious to the Lord and the human authorities He places over them acts independently and thinks he/she is self-sufficient. Only God is self-sufficient and all human beings are dependent upon the Lord and others for help. Human beings are fallen creatures who are born needy, dependent, insufficient, and weak, yet our culture looks upon these characteristics with disdain. For a Christian, however, these four terms should not be offensive but must be embraced because a committed follower of Christ needs the Lord, is dependent upon the Lord and others, is sufficient only in Christ, and relies upon the strength of the Holy Spirit. Self-sufficiency is not the primary goal of Christianity because God wants His children to recognize that each of us is dependent upon others in the body of Christ, with Christ as the head of that body. Think of a person who has a neuromuscular disease. The head no longer controls the hand and other parts of the body. The body of Christ often acts like it has muscular dystrophy or Parkinson's disease but this must not be so! The body of Christ must submit its "limbs" to Christ and not act independently of the Head. True Christ followers are submitted to Christ and His human authorities. True Christ followers are surrendered to Christ and they value the principle of submission along with the protection and love He provides.[19] Do you value submission? Are you submitted to a trusted Christian friend, a mentor, or a church leader?

PRAYER: "Father, remind me that you are the Lord of my life as well as my Savior. Help me to submit to you just as Jesus did when He submitted His will to yours (Luke 22:42). Help me to submit to the human authorities you have placed over me."

---

[19] Taken from *Addiction-Proof Parenting*.

Day 33
LONELINESS

> "Behold, the hour is coming, indeed it has come, when you will be scattered, each to his own home, and will leave me alone. Yet I am not alone, for the Father is with me" (John 16:32).

Mandy sets her alarm clock to get up at 6 a.m. each day because she must leave her house by 7:30 to get to work on time. The problem is that Mandy's clock has a "snooze button" that gives her nine more minutes of sleep before sounding the alarm again. Mandy can push the "snooze button" as often as she chooses and she usually pushes it 3 or 4 times every morning. Needless to say, Mandy ignores her alarm clock at its first ring choosing to sleep in and she ends up being late to work each day that she does.

<u>POINT TO PONDER</u>: *Loneliness is like an alarm clock that signals you that you need to spend time with the Lord in prayer and Bible reading to foster an intimate relationship of knowing Him (1 John 5:20). Do not ignore your lonely feelings and neglect spending time in fellowship with Christ.*

Loneliness is not good for anyone, especially an addict. In fact, the first time the Lord said, "It is *not* good..." was in Genesis 2:18: **"Then the LORD God said, 'It is not good that the man should be alone; I will make him a helper fit for him.'"** God saw that the man was lonely so He gave him his wife for companionship and to be his helper. If you are alone or simply feel lonely, you may not have another human being to whom you can turn, but you can always turn to the Lord. You can pray to Him anytime and He is available to listen. You can read His Word any time and

He will speak to you by His Spirit through the Bible. Your relationship with God is available twenty-four hours every day so take advantage of it. Jesus escaped from the cares of this life to be with the Father in prayer. Also, in John 16:32 (above), we see that every one of Jesus' followers abandoned Him out of fear for their own lives. Matthew 26:56b tells the same account, saying: **"Then all the disciples left him and fled."** Christ knows your loneliness because He experienced it and He has compassion for you. Let your feelings of loneliness be an alarm to alert you to your need for the fellowship of others and the fellowship of Christ. You can join with the psalmist as he prayed in Psalm 25:16-17: **"Turn to me and be gracious to me, for I am lonely and afflicted. The troubles of my heart are enlarged; bring me out of my distresses."**

PRAYER: "Father, I confess I am lonely. I ask you to send a Christian friend or someone to encourage me and to spend time with me so that I might have sweet fellowship with them and with you. I also ask you to speak to me through your Word now to reveal yourself to me so that I might have strength to do your will today for your glory."

Day 34
BALANCING THE TRUTH IN LOVE

"So that we may no longer be children, tossed to and fro by the waves and carried about by every wind of doctrine, by human cunning, by craftiness in deceitful schemes. Rather, speaking the truth in love, we are to grow up in every way into him who is the head, into Christ, from whom the whole body, joined and held together by every joint with which it is equipped, when each part is working properly, makes the body grow so that it builds itself up in love" (Ephesians 4:14-16).

Tightrope walkers often stretch their arms out perpendicular to the rope they are walking on to provide more balance. Stretched out arms cause the center of body mass to be moved out which gives more stability and balance to the walker. Both arms are needed for effective balance; otherwise, with just one arm extended, the tightrope walker will fall to one side.

POINT TO PONDER: God has provided His truth in love to hearers of His Word and His Spirit. Both the Word and the Spirit are needed for proper balance. Likewise, the truth must be balanced by grace (John 1:14) or a person will fall to one side. Strive to be balanced in your approach to truth and grace. Always present the truth in love to others but also abound in the grace you have been given (2 Corinthians 8:7).

Do you ever stop to realize how easily we are deceived and tempted to sin, by giving in to addiction and idolatrous desires? You may even see a connection between your behavior and that of a spoiled child who wants to have his own way. When this happens you need the fellowship of other Christian people and they need to be people who "speak the truth in love" to you so that you "grow up" spiritually to become more like Jesus. God wants you to know His truth for salvation and spiritual growth that is only found in His Word, the Bible. Be cautious not to believe the lies of the world and of Satan. John 8:31-32 says: **"So Jesus said to the Jews who had believed in him, 'If you abide in my word, you are truly my disciples, and you will know the truth, and the truth will set you free.'"** Choose to spend time with friends who love God's Word, know God's Word, do God's Word, and speak God's Word to you in love. You do not need so-called "worldly wisdom" because it will only confuse you, limit your spiritual growth, and bring more doubt into your relationship with Christ. James 1:6-8 says that doubting Christ causes instability: **"But let him ask in faith, with no doubting, for the one who doubts is like a wave of the sea that is driven and tossed by the wind. For that person must not suppose that he will receive anything from the Lord; he is a double-minded man, unstable in all his ways."** Trust God today by faith in the truth of God's Word.

PRAYER: "Lord, I want to have stability in my life today. Help me to trust in you by reading your Word and doing your Word in my life. Surround me with strong Christians who know and speak the truth in love so that I am not swayed by the lies of this world."

Day 35
PRIDE AND SELF-PITY

"One's pride will bring him low, but he who is lowly in spirit will obtain honor" (Proverbs 29:23).

One of my favorite books in the Bible is Esther. In that book, Haman is a man full of pride and hatred for the Jews. One day the king asked Haman how best he could honor someone special. Haman did not know that the king was referring to Mordecai, a Jew who years earlier had saved the king's life. Further, Haman had been plotting to have Mordecai hanged and the Jews sold into slavery. Since Haman did not know who the person was that the king wished to honor he naturally assumed it was himself. Esther 6:3 states: **"So Haman came in, and the king said to him, 'What should be done to the man whom the king delights to honor?' And Haman said to himself, 'Whom would the king delight to honor more than me?'"** *In the end, when his plot was exposed, Haman was executed by hanging upon the very gallows that he had constructed as a plan to kill his enemy, Mordecai.*

POINT TO PONDER: Haman's pride fed his hatred and his focus upon himself ended up blinding him to the truth and the reality around him.

Pride is like the flu virus that attacks your immune system and weakens your entire body. Pride is blinding. You need a trusted Christian friend to point out your blind spots of pride. Pride is deadly and brings destruction according to Proverbs 16:18: **"Pride goes before destruction, and a haughty spirit before a fall."** God hates our sinful pride because it destroys us as the Lord Himself says in Proverbs

8:13: "The fear of the LORD is hatred of evil. Pride and arrogance and the way of evil and perverted speech I hate." Pride sometimes comes in the form of self-pity which I call "pride in reverse." Self-pity is too much focus on self. It is a focus on what we are not getting and what we think we should get. It is the thought that "I deserve better." These thoughts are lies of the world and they breed more self-pity. The root of the problem is pride though it manifests in other ways like discontentment, hurt, bitterness, and anger. When you are feeling these emotions in a sinful way, you will always find pride at the root of it. How am I being prideful right now? What do I want that I am not getting? How am I mired in self-pity? The antidote to self-pity and pride is a heart filled with thankfulness and contentment with what your sovereign Lord has provided to you. Be thankful.

PRAYER: "Father, remind me today of your faithfulness, love, compassion, and gifts to me so that I might not be mired in self-pity and pride, but be humble, grateful, and passionate for you."

Day 36
LUST OF FLESH, LUST OF EYES, PRIDE OF LIFE

> "Do not love the world or the things in the world. If anyone loves the world, the love of the Father is not in him. For all that is in the world—the desires of the flesh and the desires of the eyes and pride in possessions—is not from the Father but is from the world. And the world is passing away along with its desires, but whoever does the will of God abides forever" (1 John 2:15-17).

If the Lord asked you right now in a dream, "Ask for whatever you want and I shall give it to you," what would you ask for? On our best day, most of us would ask for something material like a winning lottery ticket or a new car. Others might ask for a spouse, children, physical healing, or a difficult situation to be removed from our lives. These prayer requests might be considered good if you have the right heart behind them, but the Lord was particularly pleased with His newly-appointed King of Israel, Solomon, in 1 Kings 3:5. When the Lord told him: "Ask what I shall give you," Solomon asked for wisdom and discernment so that he could serve God and God's people, Israel.

POINT TO PONDER: Why did Solomon's prayer please the Lord so much? Because Solomon's focus was not on his own temporal desires for money and "happiness" in this life, but he was focused upon God's Plan to be a blessing to His people, and it reflected an eternal mindset (1 Kings 3:10-14). Because the Lord was so pleased, He answered Solomon's request for wisdom and additionally gave Him honor and great riches.

Do you have a worldly focus or a heavenly focus? Things that are eternal must be most important to you. Those "things" are human souls and your relationship with Christ. When you focus upon your relationship with Christ, the Holy Spirit will produce fruit in your life according to Galatians 5:22-23: **"But the fruit of the Spirit is love, joy, peace, patience, kindness, goodness, faithfulness, gentleness, self-control; against such things there is no law."** These fruit are spiritual and provide blessings in this life for you. Wouldn't you like more love in your life? Wouldn't you like to have more joy and peace in your life? One of the keys to producing spiritual fruit is to overcome the lust of the flesh, the lust of the eyes, and the pride of life. Our fallen, sin-cursed humanity is wired with a sinful nature that desires to please the flesh and feed our pride. It is good to know that although our Savior was also tempted by Satan to feed His earthly flesh in a sinful manner, Jesus had a heavenly focus (read Matthew 4:1-11). If you do not have a heavenly focus and instead focus upon your own selfish desires, you will choose to sin, but you can be like Christ according to Galatians 2:20: **"It is no longer I who live, but Christ who lives in me. And the life I now live in the flesh I live by faith in the Son of God, who loved me and gave himself for me."** To be like Christ in overcoming these temptations, you must cultivate your heart's desires to be in agreement with Him by learning the Word of God for yourself, being obedient to it, and speaking His Words of truth rather than believing the lies of Satan. That is exactly how Jesus overcame all three temptations in Matthew 4:1-11. You can, too.

PRAYER: "Father, empower me today to overcome the lust of my flesh, the lust of my eyes, and the pride of life, just as Jesus overcame the devil by speaking the truth of Your Word."

Day 37

THE FIRST COMMANDMENT

"You shall have no other gods before me"
(Exodus 20:3).

The story is told of man who owned a white dog and a black dog. Someone asked him, "Which dog is more loyal to you?" The man answered, "The one I feed the most."

<u>POINT TO PONDER</u>: *As a Christian, you have within you both the indwelling of the Holy Spirit and the old sinful habits of your flesh. Whichever one you feed the most will be the one that works through you to define you. Will you be known as fleshly and selfish or as Spirit-filled? Which nature will you serve: your flesh or the Holy Spirit within you?*

Any addiction violates the first commandment in Exodus 20:3 (see above). Often, other commandments are violated as well, but the focus today is on this first commandment. Scripture tells us that God is a jealous God but that does not mean He is jealous OF us. God is jealous FOR us. There is a difference. God created our hearts with an appetite for worship, and He is to be the object of that worship. Therefore, when we are caught in active addiction, we are pursuing temporary pleasures at all cost, which is worshiping the wrong person: ourselves! We were created by Him to worship Him alone and nothing else — not even ourselves or our strong desires of the flesh.

Remember that you are a soul first and a physical body second. We often put it the other way around. Focus your priorities upon feeding your soul and not the bodily appetites of your flesh. God wants us to worship Him with everything we have and in everything we do. Did you know you can worship God at your work? You can worship Him—which simply means to honor and reverence Him—in everything you do. 1 Corinthians 10:31 says that you can worship God even when you eat or drink so you definitely can worship Him at work, at home, at school, at church, or at the grocery store. Relationally, the Lord wants you to honor the authorities in your life as unto Him. Since He placed them over you, He wants your submission to them to be as though you are submitting to Him in person. Worshiping God always involves submission. Out of your deep reverence, respect, and devotion to Him, you are to show Him how worthy He is to receive honor, glory, and adoration from you by submitting to His will and not your own will (Luke 22:42).

PRAYER: "Father, make me a worshipper of you alone today in all that I think, say, and do. Change my will to your will, Lord. Let it be pleasing to you and bring glory to your Name."

Day 38
NOAH AND LOT

"Noah began to be a man of the soil, and he planted a vineyard. He drank of the wine and became drunk and lay uncovered in his tent" (Genesis 9:20-21).

A Christian man married an unbeliever despite warnings from his parents and from the Bible (2 Corinthians 6:14). He refused to heed the warning against being unequally yoked with an unbeliever and was tormented his entire life by the constant discord in their marriage. Sadly, this man's sinful choice did not affect him alone. His children grew up watching the conflict between their parents and all of them chose to stay away from church and the Lord because they concluded that Christianity was divisive. Even more tragically, the man's grandchildren never knew the Lord or even attended church. The consequences for not marrying in the Lord and raising his children in spiritual unity affected many generations.

<u>POINT TO PONDER</u>: *Many souls were lost in part because of this Christian man's one-time rebellious choice to marry an unbeliever. This one-time decision for which he was responsible led to an undermining of his faith with devastating consequences for his descendants.*

You might only know of Noah as the man who built the ark and was saved from the great Flood that God sent to judge the earth. But did you know that Noah was the first person recorded for an act of drunkenness in the Bible? Sadly, it is true and his one-time choice of drunkenness led to the additional sin and shame of his nakedness, which led to devastating consequences that affected his children and grandchildren for many years following. (Genesis 9:24-25). Noah's grandchildren, great-grandchildren, and their descendants were cursed by this one-time choice to sin in drunkenness because the Canaanites plagued the Israelites for many years and were slaves to their brothers. Another man, Lot, was responsible for being drunk with wine on two occasions even though his daughters had planned to get their father drunk with wine so that they would become pregnant. Lot's drunkenness and his daughters' sinful plan led to sexual sins with his own daughters (Genesis 19:30-38).

The children produced by Lot's two sinful episodes of drunkenness and subsequent sexual sin became known as the Ammonites and the Moabites, who plagued the children of Israel for hundreds of years. These men were not "alcoholics" with lifelong diseases; they simply made a volitional choice to sin by the excessive drinking of wine. These willful choices led to problems for thousands of people including their own families over a span of hundreds of years. Sometimes, we underestimate the power of sin and the specific sin of drunkenness. Sin affects not only us but our families and other loved ones. God knows the effect that sin has upon others and it grieves Him. The good news about all of this sin is that God forgives sinners and the writer in 2 Peter 2:5-9 considered both Noah and Lot as righteous: **"If he did not spare the ancient world, but preserved Noah, a herald of righteousness, with seven others, when he brought a flood upon the world of the ungodly; if by turning the cities of Sodom and Gomorrah to ashes he condemned them to extinction, making them an example of what is going to happen to the ungodly; and if he rescued righteous Lot, greatly distressed by the sensual conduct of the wicked (for as that righteous man lived among them day after day, he was tormenting his righteous soul over their lawless** deeds that he saw and heard); then the Lord knows how to rescue the godly from trials, and to keep the unrighteous under punishment until the day of judgment." Despite their terrible sins, God considered both of these men as *righteous* because He covered their sins with the blood of Christ since God forgives all *repentant* sinners of their sins through Christ. The character of God to forgive wayward sinners should give you and me great hope today.

PRAYER: "Father, I repent of my sins. I thank you that my sins are forgiven and that you have imputed my sins to Jesus on the cross and have imputed His righteousness to me. I ask you to lessen the consequences of my sins. For those consequences that cannot be lessened, I ask you to help me to walk in your grace trusting you will bring good from my bad choices (Genesis 50:20; Romans 8:28)."

·

Day 39

Repentance and Forgiveness

> **"Pay attention to yourselves! If your brother sins, rebuke him, and if he repents, forgive him, and if he sins against you seven times in the day, and turns to you seven times, saying, 'I repent,' you must forgive him"** (Luke 17:3-4).

Hotels usually have accommodations for adjoining rooms, separated by two connecting doors. When one door is opened, access to the adjoining room is barred unless the occupant of the other room unlocks their door. Both doors must be opened for guests at the hotel to have complete access and intimacy.

POINT TO PONDER: In our illustration, forgiveness and repentance are each represented by the doors in this hotel. Both doors must be opened for true intimacy and real relationships to heal, grow, and develop trust.

Forgiveness is an often misunderstood concept for many reasons, but one of them is that there are two Greek words for forgiveness. The first word for forgiveness is what I call the "forgiveness of the heart" as pictured in Ephesians 4:32: **"Be kind to one another, tenderhearted, forgiving one another, as God in Christ forgave you."** You can have a tender heart of forgiveness toward anyone. In fact, Jesus had this heart when He prayed in Luke 23:34: **"Father, forgive them, for they know not what they do."** The soldiers and people at the foot of the cross were not interested in His gift of forgiveness at that moment in their lives; therefore, relationally, He did not say to them, "I forgive you." Instead, He prayed to the Father asking the Father to forgive them. Sometimes, you must do the same as Jesus. Pray and ask the Father to forgive those who have hurt you and are not interested in being forgiven by you because **"they know not what they do."**

The second word for forgiveness is the transactional type of forgiveness that occurs between two *willing* persons. The key word is "willing." Both persons must be willing to do their part in this transactional moment in their relationship. One person must be willing to forgive and the other person must be willing to repent and desire forgiveness. Let's take this meaning further. Does God forgive unwilling, unrepentant, and unbelieving persons who fail to acknowledge their sin and need for Jesus as Savior? The standard Christian answer is "no" since God sends these persons into the second death (Revelation 21:8) which is to spend an eternity in conscious torment in the lake of fire (Revelation 20:14-15). God alone is the Creator and Righteous Judge of all people, not you or me, so He alone can determine the eternal destination of His created persons. Just as the Lord forgives, we are to forgive. When someone repents, we forgive them (Luke 17:3 above). Our forgiveness is not to be conditional, but is to be granted each time the person comes to us repenting, even if seven times in one day! Ouch! If the person refuses to repent, we must still forgive them in our hearts and pray for them. The relational, transactional act of forgiving is demonstrated only when both doors are open to repentance and forgiveness. This is in accordance with the principle that God forgives *repentant* sinners.[20]

PRAYER: "Father, help me to better understand your forgiveness of me when I repent. Enable me to forgive others with a heart of forgiveness whether or not they repent. When they do repent, help me to be gracious like you and forgive them of their wrongs against me."

---

[20] Thanks to Norris Anderson, who taught me this concept of the two types of forgiveness in a Sunday school curriculum he authored entitled "God's Clock" available at www.thechurchcalledlittle.org

Day 40

The First Commandment in the New Testament

"And he said to him, "You shall love the Lord your God with all your heart and with all your soul and with all your mind. This is the great and first commandment" (Matthew 22:37-38).

Mathew D. Staver was led by the Lord to start a ministry called Liberty Counsel in 1989. For ten years, he worked full-time in a law firm and part-time in Liberty Council. In 1999, while "hoping for a miraculous monetary gift to make the organization fully functional,"[21] he decided he had failed to trust God and to walk by faith. Mat and his wife decided to close their law firm and pursue God's passionate call to defend religious liberties and the sanctity of life even if he did not know where he would obtain funding. Today, Liberty Council is fully funded by individuals, churches, and organizations and supports a staff of 28 full-time workers and 20 interns. Liberty Council is called to "educate, motivate, and equip Christians" to protect the U.S. from the serious threats against our liberties.

POINT TO PONDER: *What is the Lord calling you to do today for His glory? Maybe it is not as dramatic as Mat Staver's call. Maybe the Lord simply wants you to share your faith with a lost soul, to give your talents to a cause for His glory, or to pray for and help the impoverished. Whatever it may be, do it today as your first priority with all of your heart, soul, and mind with the goal that the Lord be glorified through your obedience to Him.*

---

[21] Power for Living, January 31, 2010. p. 5

Exodus 20:3 is a command of God stating: **"You shall have no other gods before me."** Jesus acknowledged this command in His statement in Matthew 22:37-38: **"And he said to him, "You shall love the Lord your God with all your heart and with all your soul and with all your mind. This is the great and first commandment."** In other words, if Exodus 20:3 tells us what not to do, then Jesus in Matthew 22:37-38 tells us what we should do! These two commands essentially reflect the same heart of Christ. However, the heart of addiction is a focus upon pleasing oneself more than pleasing God and is a violation of the first commandment given in Exodus 20:3. Likewise, the heart of addiction is a failure to love God with everything you have and everything you are (Matthew 22:37-38). The greatest tragedy I find in my experiences as an addiction counselor is the wasted talents and gifts of addicts who could use those abilities for good and the benefit of others, but choose to squander them instead. Addicts tend to have sensitive hearts and are much needed in the body of Christ today. Jesus wants you to give your all to Him today for His glory and to advance His kingdom.

PRAYER: "Lord, show me the abilities you have given me and teach me to use them for your glory and for the benefit of others."

Day 41

PRAYER, BIBLE READING, DISCIPLINE, AND THE FRUIT OF THE SPIRIT

> **"Have nothing to do with irreverent, silly myths. Rather train yourself for godliness; for while bodily training is of some value, godliness is of value in every way, as it holds promise for the present life and also for the life to come"** (1 Timothy 4:7-8).

No one who has been physically inactive wakes up one morning, decides to run a marathon, and successfully finishes the 26 mile race. Disciplined training must occur first. It begins gradually by running just a few miles each day and increases to the point where the marathon runner can run the entire distance.

POINT TO PONDER: Spiritual disciplines are no different than the physical disciplines required for running a marathon. Prayer and Bible reading are spiritual disciplines of spending time with God in relationship with Him. Start slowly in the beginning and spend just a small portion of your day with Him with the goal of increasing the time you spend with Him daily.

Jesus said "when you pray" in Matthew 6:5, not "if you pray." Jesus assumes Christians are going to want to talk to God and He is right. But just like Peter who was asleep when Jesus asked him to pray, our flesh is weak and sometimes we do not live according to the Spirit. Mark 14:37-38 explains, **"And he came and found them sleeping, and he said to Peter, 'Simon, are you asleep? Could you not watch one hour? Watch and pray that you may not enter into temptation. The spirit indeed is willing, but the flesh is**

weak.'" Prayer is a discipline that we must develop. When we are walking in our own strength, our prayer life will be non-existent. However, when we are weak, in need, or in crisis, then our prayer life will be vibrant because we realize our desperate need for the power of God. You must train yourself for godliness and pray at all times, not just when you are in need. Godliness here refers to learning to be more loving, joyful, peaceful, and patient. These qualities are developed by people who are "practicing" those things daily in their lives. Just as an athlete trains for an upcoming event, so should a Christian train for godliness. Then, when a crisis event occurs, the Christian is ready. Train yourself to daily read your Bible. Read in the morning to start your day "according to the cadence of the King and not the drum beat of the world."[22] Begin your day in God's Word so that you hear Him speak to you. Then, pray and speak to Him. As you develop this discipline in your life, your relationship with Christ will grow, and the fruit of the Spirit will be produced more abundantly in your life (Galatians 5:22-23).

PRAYER: "Father, thank you for your Word and how it speaks to me by your Spirit. Produce through me today your fruit of the Holy Spirit so that I might be a better representative of you."

---

[22] Pastor Harry Reeder coined this expression.

Day 42
THE PURPOSE OF DRUGS

> **"No longer drink only water, but use a little wine for the sake of your stomach and your frequent ailments"** (1 Timothy 5:23).

> **"Give strong drink to the one who is perishing, and wine to those in bitter distress; let them drink and forget their poverty and remember their misery no more"** (Proverbs 31:6-7).

The law of diminishing returns is an economic principle. It means that a consumable item has diminishing value the more it is consumed. In other words, the more you consume the item, the less you want of it. It is a supply and demand principle. For example, you may decide to eat one hamburger and enjoy it very much. Maybe you decide to eat a second hamburger. You eat it and enjoy it, but not as much as you did the first one. Imagine eating a third, fourth, and fifth hamburger. The law of diminishing returns states that each hamburger eaten will decrease in pleasure to the point where you may even become completely sick of eating hamburgers.

POINT TO PONDER: Addicts often use drugs for emotional pain relief. While some addicts begin using medications for the proper goal of providing temporary physical pain relief, at some point they will begin to rely upon the medications for emotional relief. However, when the medications are used excessively, the law of diminishing returns leads a person to become more dissatisfied with the drug even with increased usage. The result is tolerance and dependence upon the drug as more of it is required to bring about the desired effect. In essence, plan in your mind to use drugs only for temporary physical purposes and not for continual emotional pain relief because the medications will never satisfy you. Only Christ satisfies the soul completely.

There is a good purpose for drugs and alcohol and that is when they are used as medicine. The Lord uses medicine prescribed by a physician in our lives for two purposes: to bring forth healing (1 Timothy 5:23) and to give us pain relief (Proverbs 31:6-7). These therapeutic purposes for taking medicine are good and taking them is right in God's eyes. But when you take medicine for reasons other than those mentioned above, you are likely taking it for the wrong heart reasons. For example, if you take any medication to escape the emotional hurts and pain of this world without a physical reason, then you are likely taking the medication with a wrong heart motive. Examine your emotional pain and realize that God wants you to glorify Him—even in those circumstances. Too many addicts and idolaters convince themselves that they have good motives for taking medications when, in reality, God knows their hearts are in the wrong place. Medications can be a blessing from God when we are in real physical pain. However, they must not be viewed as the cure for our problems because it is only in Christ that we find lasting healing from physical, emotional, and spiritual pain.

One final note is that the Lord warns leaders in the church and in the government not to drink wine at all because it is common, ordinary, and often leads to sin. In Leviticus 10:8-11, God addressed the priestly leaders: **"And the LORD spoke to Aaron, saying, 'Drink no wine or strong drink, you or your sons with you, when you go into the tent of meeting, lest you die. It shall be a statute forever throughout your generations. You are to distinguish between the holy and the common, and** between the unclean and the clean, and you are to teach the people of Israel all the statutes that the LORD has spoken to them by Moses.'" In Proverbs 31:4-5, God addressed the leaders of the government: **"It is not for kings, O Lemuel, it is not for kings to drink wine, or for rulers to take strong drink, lest they drink and forget what has been decreed and pervert the rights of all the afflicted."** If you are a leader anywhere in anything, you would be wise to heed His Words since it will glorify Him and lead to blessing in your life.

PRAYER: "Father, help me to know my heart when I use any type of medication. Purify my heart on this issue."

Day 43

THE FIFTH COMMANDMENT

> **"Honor your father and your mother, that your days may be long in the land that the LORD your God is giving you"** (Exodus 20:12).

Ten year-old Tommy was fascinated by watching the trains near his house. His parents strongly warned him, "Son, do not ever play on or near the railroad tracks." One day, he joined some of his friends who wanted to go exploring and they ended up walking on the railroad tracks looking for old railroad spikes. They walked onto a bridge to throw rocks into the water below and they did not hear the train coming until it was too late. They were faced with one of two choices: either to jump off the bridge or be hit by the train ...

POINT TO PONDER: Children are responsible for their choices, and in the illustration above Tommy and his friends faced serious consequences for their disobedience. Parents can only instruct, admonish, discipline, and love their children, but the children must obey as an act of their will. The same is true for us; we must listen to and obey our authority figures even if we do not fully understand their instruction. We are to do so as unto the Lord Himself.

You might not realize it but almost all "addictive" thoughts, words, and behaviors violate the fifth commandment in Exodus 20:12 (see above). The fifth commandment reminds us that our first God-given authorities are our parents and it is our responsibility to honor and obey them (Ephesians 6:1). Children must learn to obey, honor, and respect their parents (or those guardians in the position of parental authority such grandparents who raise a grandchild) before they will learn to respect *other* authority figures in their lives. Those addicts who single-mindedly seek temporary pleasures of any type of "addiction" excessively find a life of pain and agony with devastating long-term consequences. Loving parental authorities know this and urge their offspring to obey the laws of the Lord so that they may live long lives and prosper. Sadly, many addictions end in death, which is a very real and permanent consequence. More sadly, some of those same addicts who experience the consequence of death in this life face the second death in the everlasting life according to Revelation 20:14b-15: **"This is the second death, the lake of fire. And if anyone's name was not found written in the book of life, he was thrown into the lake of fire."** Hell is a real place and only rebels and fools will end up there. Listen to your loving heavenly Father today and those He has placed in authority over you on this earth so that you may glorify Him, prosper, and avoid the reality of hell.

PRAYER: "Lord, empower me by your Spirit to obey my human authorities today as though I am obeying you. Thank you for protecting me from my own rebellious heart that would lead me away from you."

Day 44

HELL IS A REAL PLACE: IT CAN BE AVOIDED BY GOD'S GRACE

"And cast the worthless servant into the outer darkness. In that place there will be weeping and gnashing of teeth" (Matthew 25:30).

"I'm on a highway to hell with all of my friends!" exclaims Cedric as he sings to his parents with glee. "We are going to party hard in hell together! Don't worry about me." Devastated, Cedric's parents take him with them to talk to their pastor who tells them how deceived Cedric is about the reality of hell. The pastor says, "There are no relationships in hell, Cedric. You will be alone even from the presence of God and you will be in great agony. I don't want you to be deceived about it. I urge you to read your Bible to find out the truth about hell."

<u>POINT TO PONDER</u>: *Do you live in light of the truth of eternity? Hell and heaven are real places and are the only two options in the next life. Only those who are saved by grace through faith in the Lord Jesus Christ will enter heaven (Ephesians 2:8-9). All others will be cast into hell forever.*

There are two destinations for people's souls when they physically die, according to Matthew 25:46: **"And these will go away into eternal punishment, but the righteous into eternal life."** Only those made righteous by the blood of Christ on the cross and who place their faith in Him alone for the forgiveness of their sins will inherit eternal life. All others will inherit eternal punishment. There will be no relationships in hell where there is great darkness and pain according to Matthew 25:30b: **"In that place**

there will be weeping and gnashing of teeth." Hell is a lonely place where the felt presence of the Lord God will be absent. Souls will be consumed with themselves in hell by focusing upon their own pain and agony. It is a lonely, miserable existence and its reality is not enough to save a person. Only the love of God can save a person from hell. Hell simply gets our attention to the need for repentance and the severity of the punishment for our vile sins before a holy God.

Furthermore, no one goes to hell willingly, as the Bible says in several places that unrepentant sinners are "cast" or "thrown into hell" (Matthew 5:29; Matthew 13:42; Revelation 20:15). In other words, souls will be thrust into hell since no one will want to "walk" into that place on their own volition when they see its reality — even though they were responsible for the choices on earth that got them thrown into hell. Hell is a real place, not designed to lead people to repentance because there is no repentance in hell. It is an eternal destination of punishment and that truth must motivate us to share the Gospel of the love of God to forgive any person of their sins through Jesus Christ. Otherwise, Revelation 21:8 tells us: **"But as for the cowardly, the faithless, the detestable, as for murderers, the sexually immoral, sorcerers, idolaters, and all liars, their portion will be in the lake that burns with fire and sulfur, which is the second death."** All impenitent idolaters will anguish in hell forever. If you are struggling with what the world calls "addiction," but the Bible calls the sin of idolatry, there is real hope according to 1 Corinthians 6:9-11: **"Do you not know that the unrighteous will not inherit the kingdom of God? Do not be deceived: neither the sexually immoral, nor idolaters, nor adulterers, nor men who practice homosexuality, nor thieves, nor the greedy, nor drunkards, nor revilers, nor swindlers will inherit the kingdom of God. And such were some**

of you. But you were washed, you were sanctified, you were justified in the name of the Lord Jesus Christ and by the Spirit of our God" (emphasis mine). This passage of Scripture was written to redeemed sinners who were once drunkards and idolaters but who have been transformed by the power of Christ. **"And such were some of you"** in verse 11 above should be music to your ears if you are a believer in Christ Jesus today!

PRAYER: "Father God, transform me by your power and grace to repent of my sins and to trust in Your Son alone as my Savior and only hope. Thank you for saving me from the horrible eternal destination I acknowledge that I deserve, but by your grace and mercy I am delivered from. Help me to lead others to you so that they will be forgiven of their sins, also."

Day 45
WHAT IS SELF-CONTROL?

"But the fruit of the Spirit is love, joy, peace, patience, kindness, goodness, faithfulness, gentleness, self-control; against such things there is no law. And those who belong to Christ Jesus have crucified the flesh with its passions and desires. If we live by the Spirit, let us also walk by the Spirit" (Galatians 5:22-25).

A small stream flows out from a lake in northern Minnesota and winds its way northward for a few miles. As it angles to the south, it picks up volume and power until it surges toward New Orleans as the mighty Mississippi River. The Holy Spirit is like that stream in the life of a committed Christian. It is the source of God's power in your life.

<u>POINT TO PONDER</u>: *Just as man has no control over the flow of water from Lake Itasca, we truly have no control over self. The Holy Spirit is the source of control and you are the object of His control. Yield your will to His will so that He can work through you to produce His fruit of the Spirit (Galatians 5:22-23).*

The biblical concept of self-control is different from the world's understanding of self-control. For the Christian, "self" is under the control of the Holy Spirit. In the world's eyes, self is in control, but there is no such thing as "willpower" in the flesh. The Christian needs the "will of God power" provided by Christ who dwells inside a "born again" believer. The Holy Spirit must be in control of your life to overcome an addiction and the Holy Spirit must renew the thinking in your mind for you to be transformed into the likeness of Christ. Therefore, the Holy Spirit must be in control of "self" as the Holy Spirit provides the power required. A Spirit-controlled life will produce spiritual fruit in and through you (Galatians 5:22-23). Nevertheless, do not forget the role that God's Word plays in a Spirit-filled life. The Holy Spirit works in partnership with God's Word according to several places in the Bible (Ephesians 6:17; Colossians 3:16), including John 6:63: **"It is the Spirit who gives life; the flesh is of no avail. The words that I have spoken to you are spirit and life."** Again, your flesh, which is your "self," is of no avail and has no power. Only the Spirit gives life and His power provides you with a new spirit and life. Finally, like the psalmist, you must remember what he asked the Lord in Psalm 119:9-12: **"How can a young man keep his way pure? By living according to your word. I seek you with all my heart; do not let me stray from your commands. I have hidden your word in my heart that I might not sin against you. Praise be to you, O LORD; teach me your decrees."** Ask the Lord to control you and do not try to overcome your addiction in your own strength.

PRAYER: "Father, keep my heart and ways pure by empowering me to live according to your Word of truth. Do not let me stray from your commands. I want to read your Word and memorize it so that it is hidden in my heart that I might not sin against you. Help me in this endeavor, my Father."

About the Author

Dr. Mark E. Shaw is the Founder and President of Truth in Love Ministries, an equipping and counseling ministry which operates through local churches using an innovative team approach to ministry. Dr. Shaw desires to see local churches strengthened by teaching and equipping leaders and called lay persons to competently provide shepherding care for God's "flock" of children (1 Peter 5:2) and by speaking the truth in love to one another (Ephesians 4:15).

Dr. Shaw earned both a Doctor of Ministry in Biblical Counseling and a Master of Arts in Biblical Studies from Birmingham Theological Seminary. He also obtained a Master of Science in Educational Psychology from Florida State University, and a Bachelor of Arts in Psychology from the University of South Alabama.

He has held biblical counseling certification with the National Association of Nouthetic Counselors (NANC) since 2002, and has been a certified Master's Level Addiction Professional (MLAP) with the Alabama Association of Drug and Alcohol Addiction since 1999.

For nearly two decades, he has supervised and trained counselors in marriage and family counseling, addictions counseling, and most recently in biblical counseling. In addition to counseling in the local church, he has worked as a director and counselor in outpatient clinics, crisis residential programs, intensive outpatient programs, residential rehabilitation programs, and inpatient adolescent group homes. He has witnessed the transforming and reconciling power of the Lord Jesus Christ in the lives of the many people he has served over the years.

Dr. Shaw's familiarity with biblical truths and the fallacies of many psychological theories enables him to have a unique perspective to frequently speak the truth in love to individuals, married couples, and families. Dr. Shaw and his wife, Mary, have four children and reside near Birmingham, Alabama.

MORE RESOURCES BY MARK SHAW

Divine Intervention – Hope and Help for Families of Addicts

The Heart of Addiction – A Biblical Perspective
 The Heart of Addiction Workbook

Addiction-Proof Parenting
 Publication date: September, 2010

Hope and Help Booklets

 Hope and Help Through Biblical Counseling
 Hope and Help for Marriage
 Hope and Help for Husbands and Fathers
 Hope and Help for Gambling
 Hope and Help for Video Game, TV & Internet Addiction
 Hope and Help for Self-Injurers and Cutters

All available at Focus Publishing, 1.800.913.6287
www.focuspublishinging.com

In the Greater Birmingham, AL area you can
reach Mark Shaw at Truth in Love Ministries

Truth in Love Ministries
P.O. Box 367 • Clay, AL 35048

205-910-0085 • 205-910-9221

www.histruthinlove.org
markshaw@histruthinlove.org